Exmouth

)ance is a groundbreaking
-and beyond. The primal
nnovative fusion of ecsta-

:tive and highly original,
ijesty of the old ways and
illennium. Learn how to
: spirit within the mask.
iscover new ways to com-
old gods.

)ance reveals an exciting,
irs of personal experience
) Wicca, this book unveils
nd other techniques that

About the Authors

EVAN JOHN JONES first came into contact with Witchcraft and the occult during the 1960s, a time of great change in Britain which stemmed from the repeal in 1951 of the Witchcraft Act. By 1960, Witchcraft as a subject was firmly placed in the practical mind. His interest in Witchcraft both in theory and as a practical system of belief has never wavered. Ex-regular Army and an engineer by profession, he was later forced by ill health to retire. He is married and now lives in Brighton, not far from the Downs where he first experienced the magic of the Witches' circle. He is also the author of *Witchcraft: A Tradition Renewed* and a contributor to Llewellyn's *Witchcraft Today* series.

CHAS S. CLIFTON lives in the southern Colorado foothills. In addition to editing Llewellyn's Witchcraft Today series, he wrote *The Encyclopedia of Heresies and Heretics* (ABC-Clio, 1992) and also teaches university writing classes. He is a contributing editor of *Gnosis*, and his column, "Letters from Hardscrabble Creek," is carried in several Pagan magazines. He holds a master's degree in religious studies from the University of Colorado.

To Write to the Authors

If you wish to contact the authors or would like more information about this book, please write to the authors in care of Llewellyn Worldwide, and we will forward your request. Both the authors and publisher appreciate hearing from you and learning of your enjoyment of this book and how it has helped you. Llewellyn Worldwide cannot guarantee that every letter written to the authors can be answered, but all will be forwarded. Please write to:

Llewellyn Worldwide Ltd.
P.O. Box 64383, Dept. K373–5, St. Paul, MN 55164-0383, U.S.A.
Please enclose a self-addressed, stamped envelope for reply, or $1.00 to cover costs.
If outside the U.S.A., enclose international postal reply coupon.

SACRED MASK
SACRED DANCE

Llewellyn's Craft Series

SACRED MASK

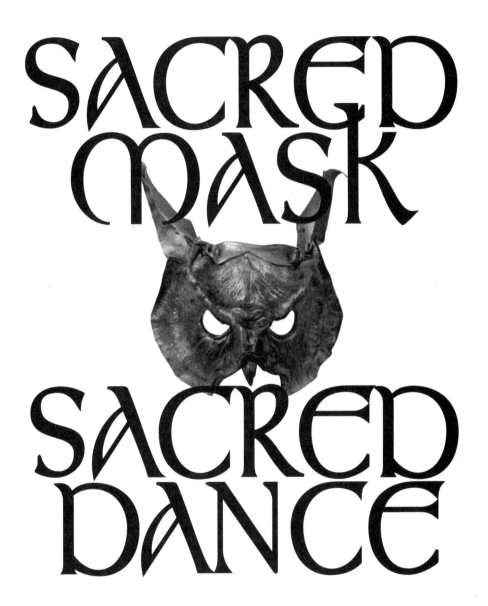

SACRED DANCE

Evan John Jones
with Chas S. Clifton

1997
Llewellyn Publications
St. Paul, Minnesota 55164-0383, U.S.A.

FIRST EDITION
First Printing, 1997

Cover design by Anne Marie Garrison
Cover photos by Robin Larsen and Wendy Crowe,
    mask courtesy of Sears Eldredge; mask maker, Jorge Añón
Illustrations by Carrie Westfall and Tom Grewe
Interior design and editing by Connie Hill
Photos by Robin Larsen, Malcolm Brenner, Evan John Jones, Chas S. Clifton,
    Karen St. Pierre, Stephen Larsen, Terry Dimant, Wendy Crowe, Jeff Farnum,
    Laura Prince

Library of Congress Cataloging-in-Publication Data
Jones, Evan John. 1936–
    Sacred mask, sacred dance / Evan John Jones with Chas S. Clifton. — 1st ed.
    p.   cm. —
    Includes bibliographical references.
    ISBN 1–56718–373–5 (trade paper)
    1. Masks — Religious aspects. 2. Dance — Religious aspects. 3. Witchcraft.
4. Shamanism. 5. Paganism. I. Clifton, Chas S. II. Title
    BF1572.M37   1997
    291.3'7—dc21   96–40945
                                                                        CIP

Llewellyn Publications
A Division of Llewellyn Worldwide, Ltd.
St. Paul, Minnesota, 55164-0383, U.S.A.

Acknowledgements

In memory of Robert Cochrane and to Valerie for all her help. Also to Jane, and with special thanks to Doreen Valiente.

—EJJ

My special thanks to Gwyneth Cathyl-Bickford, Judy Harrow, and to Kate Slater for sharing their invaluable experience with masking and trancing, and for looking things up in Y *Geiriadur Mawr*. Thanks also to Martin Anthony and members of the mask-making workshop at the 1995 Front Range Pagan Festival.

—CSC

Other Books by the Authors

by Evan John Jones

Witchcraft: A Tradition Renewed
Co-authored with Doreen Valiente (published by Robert Hale Ltd., 1990)

by Chas Clifton

The Encyclopedia of Heresies and Heretics (published by ABC-Clio, 1992)

edited by Chas Clifton

Witchcraft Today, Book One: The Modern Craft Movement
Witchcraft Today, Book Two: Rites of Passage
Witchcraft Today, Book Three: Witchcraft & Shamanism
Witchcraft Today, Book Four: Living Between Two Worlds
(all published by Llewellyn Publications)

Dedicated to

Robert Cochrane and

Bill and Bobbie Gray

CONTENTS

The Masked Rites
of Tubal Cain

The shamanistic and ritual methods described in this book were not handed down through a family or group tradition. Far from it—they started as experiments and gradually expanded and grew as the group of British Pagans of which I am a part realized just how useful a working tool they could be. After talking to one or two other groups that we knew of who were like-minded and who practiced something of a similar nature, we found that, instead of discovering something new, what we had done was to rediscover an ancient concept and way of working. Not only are these rites not an inherited tradition passed on to me, they are not like the rites we had first practiced years ago. For more than a decade now, we have refined their shamanistic elements through trial and error, defining them and giving them a specific shape and form.

Another interesting thing we found when talking to other groups was that even though the basic techniques and approach were the same, the actual working methods were flexible, allowing groups to develop their own individual style and mythos while remaining within the framework of the original concept. Having realized this, the next thing we had to do was to flesh out what we had worked on and create a formal working method, symbolism, and mythos—what we now call "The Masked Rites of Tubal Cain."

In her foreword to my first book, *Witchcraft: A Tradition Renewed*, Doreen Valiente commented on the fact that the rituals therein were more shamanistic than anything else. Likewise, in the chapter titled "Robert Cochrane, Magister" in her own book, *The Rebirth of Witchcraft*, she stressed the shamanistic nature of Cochrane's rituals. She is quite right, and Doreen realized this before we ever did. To us it was simply one of our ways of working.

When we examined our concept in a historical sense to establish its origin and growth, we concluded that trance-state magic is simply as old as humankind itself and that it was at one time universal. As the perceived visions of the Goddess and the Old Gods became more formalized with time, the shamanistic elements of any religion either died out or became more specialized, as in the case of the Nordic shamanistic tradition and faith.

In our case, however, we decided that there would be little point in blending the coven workings and the masked workings. Of course, they can be blended if *all* the members of the group are not only willing but suited to this sort of working, but even though the faculty of first-state trance is part of everyone's genetic heritage, to use it in a shamanistic, priestly way requires a special sort of person. Not all Witches are willing to commit themselves to

this. Therefore, if covens keep the masked rites separate from the coven rites, they will avoid this clash of interests. *The coven rites and workings must always come first.* That way everyone in the group feels that they are first and foremost coven members. The masked trance rites may be treated as a "mystery within a mystery," but those who take part in them are no "higher" in grade than anyone else in the coven. If this distinction can be understood, then there should be no trouble in the idea of working the masked trance rites being accepted by everyone.

Some people might question the idea of reintroducing trance workings into modern Witchcraft, saying that they do not fit with the more celebratory path that much modern Craft practice tends to take. I can only say that the Craft is strong enough to absorb many ideas, and to try and exclude any form of shamanistic working from the faith would in a sense be cutting it off from some of the roots from which it sprang.

Shamanism did not fail the Craft—far from it! Its decline was due more to the climate of opinion in Christian times. Perhaps during the Renaissance the influx of "New Learning" and hermetic occult sciences, which appealed to educated people (many of whom would have been the grand masters of their gatherings), helped bring about the demise of much of the old Anglo-Saxon tradition, and with it the shamanistic rites. At the same time, more revived Greco-Roman mythology and traditions were introduced, and these helped form the basis of today's Witchcraft.

Just as magic and the faith stood at a crossroads centuries ago, many of us today feel the Craft stands at another crossroads leading to new interpretations of the old ways. No longer is Witchcraft just Witchcraft; it has now become "Earth Magic," bringing new ideas, new thinking, and new concepts. So why not bring back the old ideas of a trance-based shamanistic Witchcraft? After all, there is a long historical precedent, based on the evidence of the witch trials.

For instance, in 1598, during the Aberdeen witch trials, which resulted in the burning of twenty-four men and women, the accused Scottish witches were supposed to have gathered at the Fish Cross of the burgh, and there, under the command of "Satan," to have danced around the cross. Furthermore, some of them, including a woman named Bessie Thom, were also accused of transforming themselves into other forms. Among those listed were hares and cats. At another Scottish trial, at Alloa in 1658, the defendants were charged not only with witchcraft and shape-shifting, but,

while in the shape of cats, of murdering certain children. The odd thing was that some of the accused claimed to have entered the house in cat shape to do the killing. Others who were present testified that as far as they could see, there was no visible change in the outward appearance of these witch-cats. I will return to these two seemingly contradictory claims below.

Even though these examples were Scottish, the tradition of masked witch rites was more widespread. In 1673 Ann Armstrong, a member of a Northumberland coven, declared that at one meeting the "devil" or master of the coven changed Ann Bates into various animal forms. On the island of Guernsey, Marie Bequet claimed that when the "devil" came to her, he always transformed her into a bitch. Again and again, shape-shifting appears in the trial records. At the same time, the records reveal that not everyone at the coven gathering engaged in shape-shifting. While this is not conclusive evidence, I think it suggests the existence of a two-tier system within the coven. Some could see themselves as animals; others, while not shape-shifting themselves, could perceive the changes in their fellow coveners.

The method employed to make this change apparently was a simple one. We would expect to find an elaborate ritual accompanying the donning of the mask and robes for the animal transformation, but as the confessions show, the chanting of a simple spell or being touched by the Master and told what guise to adopt was sufficient. This simple approach was possible because there was no uninitiated congregation to impress. After all, one reason for any ritual, elaborate or otherwise, is to create the right kind of atmosphere and feeling among the worshipers—something that would be unnecessary with only coven members present.

I believe that the witch-trial evidence demonstrates that both the witches and their accusers realized that the change to an animal form was mental rather than physical. Knowing this, there would have been no reason to go into a long explanation of why and how it was accomplished. After all, the court's job was to try the accused persons for witchcraft, not to explain the whys and wherefores of the Craft. Later readers of the trial documents would come across phrases such as "so-and-so went to a meeting in the shape of a cat" and naturally think that the poor old dear was suffering from delusions, and rightly so, for changing one's shape from a human one to that of an animal through magic is physically impossible. This in turn would foster the idea that any religion whose followers claimed they could change

themselves into cats, dogs, horses, or other animals, contrary to natural law, could not amount to much. In the end, something that the old witches understood became an instrument to denigrate them with.

Only in the Victorian era was both British and Nordic pre-Christian history seriously looked at and discovered to be rich and varied, rather than crude and barbaric. It was from these abundant sources, with their gods, demigods, and heroes, that the old faith and the branch of the old faith that we call Witchcraft drew their strength.

When we re-examine the witch-trial evidence in the light of these traditions, we can begin to see how shamanism fits into Witchcraft. Shamanistic lore states that when the shaman contacts the gods, he or she does so in spirit, having first shape-shifted into a specific animal guise. As an aid in doing this, the shaman may wear a ritual costume, including a mask. The trial evidence suggests that masks were part of the ritual in certain covens, along with going to meetings in the shape of animals. The tradition suggests that the soul left the body, changed its shape, and then communicated with the gods. Those sixteenth- and seventeenth-century witch-trial judges would never have realized it, but they were dealing with the last echoes of a line of religious experience stretching back to the dawn of time, the god-seeking shamanistic trance.

For all we know, many of those former witches wearing masks would not have known just where the masks originated or what their primary use was. Instead, they probably regarded them as something worn at the meetings when they were working magic. All they were sure of was that in order to make certain spells work, they had to wear masks while doing them. Eventually the masks were used by rote rather than by understanding, because with the advent of Christianity in Anglo-Saxon England, Pagan cults were gradually suppressed. In the Scandinavian north, however, Christianity was fiercely resisted until the eleventh century, when it was finally accepted. In Iceland, according to *Burnt Njal's Saga*, it triumphed only through a peculiarly Norse combination of single combat and lawsuits. Still, such sagas and the Eddas give us insight into a Norse Paganism that shares much with the Anglo-Saxon Wotan mythos.

The original Saxon invaders of England were illiterate and would have depended on oral tradition to hand down their faith. The only written source about them comes from Welsh Christian annalists who inferred that the best place for the pagans' souls was in Hell. So strong was this anti-Saxon feeling among the Celtic Christians that, even when given the opportunity, they refused to convert the Saxons but remained isolated within their own culture, leaving missionary work first to the Irish monks of Iona. Ultimately, the Saxons were converted by Augustine of Canterbury and other missionaries sent from Rome. It is little wonder that the old Pagan English mythos received short-shrift from the Roman-trained English clerics. The last thing they would be interested in was the Pagan worship of their ancestors—far better to record the lives of English saints like Augustine and Wilfrid and their fight against the Devil and all his works.

Given this history—or rather the lack of it—the one thing I am not advocating is re-creating the past. Far from it. Let us instead create the future by using tried and tested tools from the past. As long as we do not claim that what we are doing is an exact re-creation of the old ways but an old concept shaped to suit modern ways, then a place can and should be made for shamanistic rites within Witchcraft. This book offers some first steps along the way, but the shaman's way has always been an individualistic one, and each person who elects to follow it through working with others of a like mind must find his or her own keys to the concept. May they find as much satisfaction in these rites as we have!

—Evan John Jones

Editorial Note

Throughout this book, the spellings "priest(ess)" and "god(dess)" have been used, as many Pagan writers do, as abbreviations for "priest and/or priestess" and "goddess and/or god." Readers should supply either or both genders as appropriate.

The decision of whether or not to capitalize such words as "witch," "witchcraft," "faith," and "craft" was made according to the following rule of thumb. They are capitalized when they refer to the modern, revived Neopagan religion of Witchcraft, also called Wicca, or to any of its synonyms ("the Craft," "the Old Religion," etc.) or to its followers ("modern Witches"). They are not capitalized when they refer to historic witchcraft—in other words, that still not fully understood period ranging from the late Middle Ages through the seventeenth century, when tens of thousands of persons were imprisoned or executed in western Europe and its colonies as heretical "witches." Nor are they capitalized if they are used in the unfortunate anthropological sense meaning "evil magic-worker" when translating a word from some other language.

This difference is maintained because whatever the self-image of pre-Christian Paganism or any Pagan or shamanic practices that survived the conversion to Christianity, nowadays we are more prone to define religious traditions distinctly. Since Neopagan Witchcraft is considered by its followers to be not only just a set of practices but one manifestation of Pagan religion, it therefore deserves capitalization as a proper noun. Likewise, "Pagan" is not defined negatively as "having no religion" but positively as a collective reference to a variety of polytheistic, Earth-based traditions.

All quotations from the Robert Cochrane-William Gray correspondence are verbatim, except where spelling or punctuation have been modified for American usage. I personally have seen copies of all the quoted letters, which date from the mid-1960s. Gray saved the letters and passed them on to Evan John Jones just before he died, in the hope that Jones could make some literary use of them.

—Chas S. Clifton

Introduction

The Rebirth of Masked Magic

Dionysos is not the god behind the mask. He is the mask.
Ginette Paris, *Pagan Grace*[1]

Masks obliterate the human personality with all its frail quirks, all its physiological imperfections. Made properly and used with skill on highly charged occasions, the effect on the consciousness of the celebrants can be staggering. Holes can be punched in the rational defenses, and [the wearer] can be made to know that he is, beyond any doubt, in the company of gods.
Alan Richardson, *Earth God Rising*[2]

The approaches to ritual laid out in this book go far beyond merely theatrical ideas of "ritual drama." Instead, their aim is a dramatic (in both senses of the word) form of consciousness alteration, in a Pagan religious mode. What Evan John Jones here describes as the "Masked Rites of Tubal Cain" offers modern Witches a way to inject a new element into ritual work, to go beyond the normal states of consciousness, and to awaken dormant spiritual states. These rites balance form and freedom using ancient methods. And, as both the Canadian archetypal psychologist Ginette Paris and the English occultist Alan Richardson agree, under the right circumstances, masks can be a powerful transformational tool.

The power of masked ritual is felt even when it is deliberately revived as a diluted, nonsectarian public festival, as has often happened. For example, during the nineteenth century, public masked festivities were revived (or in some cases created) throughout Europe. Imbued as they might have been with notions of cultural "progress" and "evolution," the people were also increasingly exposed to the power of the archaic world. Ironically, one vehicle for this exposure was the Christian missionary effort. Although they set out to convert the "heathens" in other countries, missionaries often brought back information about these heathens' lives to the people at home where it was linked up with the new interest in folklore studies and anthropology. Although scholars at the time were perhaps too prone to believe that all culture moved through the same progressions and, therefore, that one might see in New Guinea, for instance, a parallel to Stone Age England, this new information about other cultures had a freshening effect on the people at home.

Colonial administrators also played their part: the returned colonist who had been exposed to the "mysteries of the East (or Africa)" became a stock figure in literature. (Although his time was the early twentieth century, Gerald Gardner fit this pattern perfectly.)

Meanwhile, the nineteenth century also saw a rising interest in "roots" and cultural identity. This interest manifested in literature, art, music, and public ritual—ritual that was officially simply "folkloric," but which rapidly touched something deeper. Books, paintings, poems, and musical contributions are usually understood to have a specific creator and a specific date—not so masked rituals. The masked rituals' power is so strong that they only have to be performed for a few years to seem to be "ancient." As the French scholar Henry Pernet noted, "certain Swiss masks, whose grimacing expressions and monstrous faces were believed to be a measure of their archaism, in fact only dated to the nineteenth century...and their appearance could be traced to the vogue for the exotic that marked that century and by the knowledge of 'primitive' customs, mostly diffused by the missionaries' gazettes, which it incited."[3]

While the "official" origin story of these masked processions varies, no one needs to know it for the processions to continue and to be popular. Pernet may well have been referring to the famously grotesque hand-carved wooden masks of Loetschental, a valley in Switzerland, worn by "wild men" (*tschaeggaettae*) during the area's pre-Lenten Carnival.[4] Carnival and Christmas/New Year (the former Roman Saturnalia) remain the two most popular times for masked processions in most Christian cultures. In Romania, however, masks were sometimes part of rural funerals and weddings: here an individual changes status, whereas at New Year or Lent the secular/ sacred year itself changes.[5]

As a religious practice, however, masking goes all the way back. The famous "sorcerer" of Les Trois Frères cave in France may have been a masked dancer, or a half-man/half-beast...or both. The British Middle Stone Age stag masks mentioned in Chapter One do definitely suggest masked ritual. Still later, a masked figure appears on an Egyptian funerary temple wall dated to about 2500 B.C.E. Given the frequent portrayal of Egyptian deities as human-bodied and animal-headed, it is tempting to think that masked religious rituals were undertaken there during some eras. Public masked processions with definite Pagan religious overtones lasted in western Europe until at least the early Middle Ages, before being gradually tamed and reduced to a few specific performances. In addition, a few reports from the period of the witch trials mention masks being worn.

The "Sorcerer" from Les Trois Frères, the figure of a human wearing the head and skin of an animal.

The masked rites described in this book, however, are designed for small-group performance. Perhaps in the future they will grow into something larger and more public. However, were that to happen, it is an open question if they would still have the shamanic power that they now hold for the individuals participating in them. Experienced Witches created the rites, and presume that anyone attempting them already is familiar with the basics of self-preparation for ritual, creating sacred space, calling the Guardians of the Four Quarters, casting a circle, and so forth. Later chapters provide "scripts" for rituals that focus on specific masked beings: the divinatory rite of Squirrel, the ecstatic prophecies of Hare, and so on. Should you choose to work them, you will undoubtedly be led by the masks' power into other rites as well.

The divine aspects or god-forms presented in the following pages may be worked with because the Craft in everyday concept is polytheistic. Because there is no one source of divine authority that is not counterbalanced by another, there is less need within the Craft today to draw distinct lines between "person," "god," "spirit," "self," "inner," "outer," "here," and "there." The Witch moves in and out of different realities without necessarily judging them. Consequently, shamanically inclined Witches can benefit from incorporating masked workings into their coven or group rituals. The masks may represent different aspects within the Old Faith, becoming the faces of the minor gods and goddesses called upon within the cycle of the rites.

The *theatricality* of the masked workings is valuable to modern Witches, for much in our contemporary world works against an Earth-centered Pagan outlook. I do not mean here so much the influence of other religions as the constant ambient message that "What you see is all that there is." The greatest enemy the modern Witch faces is the internal voice that says, "You're kidding yourself. Get a life."

Witches often point to the value of ritual and the practice of either wearing robes or going naked in the sacred circle; we say these practices tell our inner selves, "Pay attention: this is important!" But the dramatic value of masked working is even stronger because it is transpersonal; we present visual messages to each other in the masks and costumes that we wear.

At the same time, the viewer responds to the mask, not to the wearer personally. Knowing this, the wearer is aware of himself or herself as a conduit of the power carried by the mask. The wearer realizes that "real life" is not only what we think it is; there is a "more real" life behind it, hard to perceive but always active. Anything we can do to touch it, to give it space to operate in our lives, to observe its manifestations (the mask, the dream, the chill up the spine, the "Freudian slip") adds to our knowledge as Witches.

In this introduction, I also would like to discuss three interrelated ideas. One is the power of the mask itself and how it reveals the psychological impoverishment of the monotheistic world view. Another is the historical religious connection between masked rituals and the Underworld (or Lower World), here visualized as the realm of the older dead and of the ancient animal powers. Third, I would like to add some thoughts about trance, although that subject is discussed in additional detail elsewhere, particularly in Chapter Four, "Reaching the Unconscious."

In traditional cultures, masks could carry many meanings. Our dominant culture's thinking on masking, however, tends to be limited to one idea only: concealment, either theatrical or criminal. Our masked heroes and super-heroes—the Lone Ranger, Batman, and the rest—were all consciously created as business enterprises, whatever archetypal connections they may make. The most famous masked dancers in America work for the Disney Corporation, and the idea of Mickey and Goofy as "culture heroes" says it all, but this sad state of affairs is only one manifestation of masking's possibilities. The masks' power wants to re-assert itself, coming as it does from that "other side" where magic lives.

Over time we have reduced the meaning of public masks for adults to only one idea: a concealing of the social persona that permits normally repressed parts of the personality to emerge. Children, of course, are allowed to wear masks for Hallowe'en, school plays, and so on, but that is just "kid stuff." (The Hallowe'en connection is obvious, but set it aside for a moment.) What we have for adults could be called the "Mardi Gras theory" of masking: for certain events, such as the New Orleans Mardi Gras festivities, the Philadelphia New Year's Mummers' Parade, or the Greenwich Village Hallowe'en parade in New York City, people are allowed to assume alternate personae or, in effect, to act out their unconscious in public. Meanwhile archaic masked workings have largely degenerated into masquerades—Carnival, Fastnacht, and

Philadelphia Mummers' Museum

Mummers parades such as the one held every New Year's Day in Philadelphia give participants an opportunity to assume a different identity. Sometimes, as here, makeup serves as a mask.

the rest, not to mention the masked balls once popular in high society.

The Latin word *persona* started out to mean nothing but "mask." In the Greek and Roman theatre, actors commonly wore masks—and they learned their parts from scrolls called *rotoli*, hence "roles." So are the Mardi Gras partiers just switching one mask for another? Or, perhaps, do maskers act out a collective unconscious? Here comes a New Orleans Mardi Gras "krewe" (or a Rio de Janeiro samba school) down the street, dressed as Zulu warriors...as eighteenth-century aristocrats in white wigs and satin...as impossibly feathered fluorescent birds... What collective unconscious is *this?*

Even though we limit the use of masks, our language carries some limiting ideas about masking: "persona," meaning a constructed presentation of the self, or "unmasking," which suggests that the mask is "false" and that whatever lies underneath it is "true." For Witches, however, unquestioned unconscious allegiance to this linguistically embedded idea is only going to make masked ritual harder. Instead, as Ginette Paris suggests, let us recognize "Dionysos, patron of actors, who invites us to play every role, tragic as well as comic, grotesque as well as solemn, with intensity, with spirit and brio. To know Dionysos, we must accept identification with the mask

instead of searching for something behind it." As ritualists, we understand that we not only "go out" but we "come back" as well. Hence, as Paris continues, "To be Dionysian, one needs not only to identify fully with the person, animal, or divinity pictured by the mask, but also to accept that this identification is never definitive and final."[6]

Masked working, like Drawing Down the Moon/Sun and other important Wiccan rituals, comes easier if we regard ourselves as psychically more fluid than the linguistic concept of "unmasking reveals the truth" permits. Other mask-using cultures, ranging from Egypt to Greenland, have seen themselves as composed of several souls. Among the traditional Inuit (Eskimo) people, well-known for their shamanism, a person consisted of a body plus several "souls."

One, the *ateq* or name soul, remained in this world after death. It gradually disappeared, but its persistence led to a prohibition (common in a number of cultures besides the Inuit) against using a dead person's name for a year. The person who foolishly used the dead person's name could be unpleasantly haunted by the *ateq*.

More important was the *tarneq*, the supernatural soul which left the body at death to travel to the Land of the Dead. Its temporary absence—except among shamans, who were trained in soul travel—would cause illness. In addition, traditional Inuit accepted the existence of smaller "souls" dwelling in the body's joints; their absences could also cause illness.[7]

Compare the Egyptian concept of the *ka*, the impermanent soul containing the individual personality, "fed" by tomb offerings, and the *ba*, the impersonal, imperishable essence.

By driving a wedge into the "monotheistic" concept of soul, these ideas help us to understand that the boundary between this world and other worlds is not fixed and impermeable. We need to drop the idea that there is some "true self" under a variety of metaphorical social "masks." Instead, we can honor the physical mask and the ritual that employs it for permitting us to accept and share the power of the "person, animal, or divinity" that it holds. Instead of hiding behind the mask, we see it as the link between ourselves and this other powerful realm.

In traditional shamanic cultures it is the role of the shaman to visit the dead, among others, and to solicit their advice. Modern shamans may also visit and retrieve aspects of an individual's soul that are "temporarily dead" and locked away due to past trauma.[8]

When modern historians and anthropologists began to study other cultures, they saw that in many instances masked figures represented the dead in two senses. They might be the individual dead or, just as likely, the dead in a larger, collective sense in which individuals are matched with appropriate god/goddesses and cultural figures. This observation links up with another observation about our own culture: one of its more powerful archaic survivals is the image of the passage of the dead through the world of the living, which surfaces in every ghost story and is reenacted each year on the last day of October.

This collective passage of the dead was once referred to as the "Wild Hunt," in the sense of mounted hunters and dogs pursuing something... or someone. In old stories, the Wild Hunt was lead by the King of the Underworld—Herla or Odin. In Romano-Celtic areas this procession of the dead might have been led by Diana the huntress or by the goddess Epona, associated with both horses and the Underworld.[9] (A popularized and Christianized American treatment of the same theme underlies the old Country and Western song "Ghost Riders in the Sky.") The theme of the Wild Hunt and its component creatures (Hound, Mare, and so on) will become one of this book's important themes.

The connection between masks and the realm of the dead refuses to die, even in this age. Consider the 1994 newspaper article that began as follows:

The living shuffled through the dark, windswept streets of Denver, praying that the spirits of the dead would join them in celebration.

"Come back, grandfather, I miss you," one called. "Viva Raul Julia!" cried another. And there was this mournful wail: "Richard Nixon, we miss you!"

The macabre marchers wound through northwest Denver, from the Pirate art gallery to Our Lady of Guadalupe Church, all the time chanting the names of dearly departed. Some faces were painted in death masks of black and white; others sprouted horns or were shrouded in blood-red veils.[10]

This masked procession happened neither at Carnival nor on New Year's Day, but at an older New Year, the first day of November, known in Hispanic cultures as *El día de los muertos*, the day of the dead. The ancient connection reasserts itself: the date, the Underworld, the masked procession, and the Goddess in a Mesoamerican aspect, the Virgin of Guadalupe.

In a parallel way, the Wiccan masked rites described here are explicitly connected with that Underworld ruled by the Goddess in her aspect as mistress of the Spiral Castle, the realm of the dead. The ultimate purpose of the masks, the dance with its symbolic connection to the turning of that celestial mill that pivots on the Pole Star, the poems and chants, is to make that journey—and to return.

The masked workings are a Mystery, of which it may be said that they may have more than one level and that these levels do not contradict one another but correspond to different levels of understanding. Consequently, when it is time to discuss the animal masks of Her "following" or retinue, they may be discussed in naturalistic, symbolic, and mythic terms. A hare is "mad" in the spring because that is its mating season; but the "madness" may also be understood as an inspired prophetic state in the dancer wearing the mask of Hare. As a Romanian writer on masks put it:

> When used as instruments of magical transformation, masks brought about actual spiritual changes in the wearer. Such changes included the alteration of identity, the loss of personality, the creation of a double personality, the inducement of a dreamlike trance. Masks could also bring about a metamorphosis or a hierophany. It was especially the prehistoric priest, and through him the faithful, who underwent such transformation.[11]

Take out the gender-specific language and the limiting reference to the "prehistoric," and you have the subject matter of this book!

The subject of trance, however, tends to be misunderstood because it is described and reported in so many different ways. For example, what one person calls "inspiration" may be described elsewhere as "possession." And "possession" itself is a loaded term: Christian writers would use it only negatively, whereas the experience of being temporarily "ridden" by a deity is actively sought out in many religions. The only unfortunate aspect about a term like "ridden," however, is that it reinforces the thinking that deity exists only outside us. In reality, in the fluidity of Wiccan thinking, divinity may be personified at one moment and experienced as a state of consciousness the next. To paraphrase a teaching given to me years ago, "If you persist in treating the gods as archetypes, they will surprise you by acting like people; and if you think of them as persons, they may manifest as archetypes."

Another way of stating this comes from Robert Gover's book on African-derived religion, *Voodoo Contra*, "Indeed, the pagan gods are such [basic] truths, for they are older than any religious scriptures and more basic than any scientific principles....Knowledge of self means knowledge of consciousness, which is the home of both pagan gods and scientific concepts."[12]

Granted that all descriptions of trance are highly individualistic, not to mention idiosyncratic, categorizing trance workings is difficult. The archaeologist J. David Lewis-Williams, whose study of southern African Bushman (San) rock carving and its relationship to the San shamans' trance journeys is summarized in Chapter Four, described three stages of trance induction.[13] The first stage involved seeing geometric images, which Lewis-Williams, coming from a materialist viewpoint, believed were simply stray signals generated by the brain. The second stage was the images' interpretation and the third a sensation of traveling down a tunnel— the image which modern teachers of "core shamanism" such as Michael Harner see as central to shamanism cross-culturally.

Another way of talking about trance used by some Witches is to divide it into three or four levels. The first level is called "enhancement trance" by some; it corresponds to the sensation many Witches report during both successful ritual and successful may include a prickling or "electric" sensation on the skin and scalp combined with a detachment from anything outside the ritual circle. The person feels calmer, more authoritative, and more tuned in to non-verbal information. (Compare the feeling that successful athletes often report that they experience during competition.) Reading a script may interfere with this altered state of consciousness; to stay in the enhancement trance, memorized se-quences of actions and words are almost essential.

A deeper stage, inspirational trance (sometimes divided into shallower and deeper levels), is marked by definite sensations of being in touch with something larger—of "being along for the ride," as it is sometimes said. The person is still aware of where he or she is, however, but some short-term memory loss may occur. Highly successful divination can also take you to this level; you have access to information, but you do not know where it is coming from. To continue the athletic comparison, this is more of a "runner's high."

At some point, this inspirational trance merges into a possession trance. Time seems to slow down, something like it seems to do during emergencies—often the kinds of emergencies in which our bodies perform at levels we are not normally capable of. When the third level is concluded, the person may feel like a loser in a barroom brawl.[14] Someone emerging from this level of trance has no memory of what she or he did and requires assistance, rest, and nourishment. The traditions that focus on possession trance, such as the Afro-Brazilian Candomblé and Umbanda or Caribbean Voodoo, always have their ritual areas set up so that exhausted dancers can rest, eat, and drink in a quiet space. These religions developed in warm countries, and as one Canadian Witch said, "A ritual happening out-of-doors in a cold and snowy environment may present an inappropriate venue for possession trance."

As further reading in this book will make clear, the masked rites can be worked at all these levels—and worked successfully. The important thing is to begin them.

—Chas S. Clifton

Notes

1. Ginette Paris, trans. Joanna Mott, *Pagan Grace: Dionysos, Hermes, and Goddess Memory in Daily Life* (Dallas: Spring Publications, 1990), 49.

2. Alan Richardson, *Earth God Rising* (St. Paul, MN: Llewellyn Publications, 1990), 80.

3. Henry Permet, *Ritual Masks: Deceptions and Revelations* (Columbia, SC: University of South Carolina Press, 1992).

4. Art Maier, "Serene valley's strange wooden masks hide their history," *The Denver Post*, December 26, 1993, 6T.

5. Romulus Vulcanescu, "Ritual Masks in European Cultures," *Encyclopedia of Religion* (New York: Macmillan, 1987).

6. Paris, 49–50.

7. Jens Peder Hart Hansen, Jørgen Meldgaard, Jørgen Nordqvist, eds., *The Greenland Mummies* (Washington: Smithsonian Institution Press, 1991 [1985], 55–56.

8. See, for example, Sandra Ingerman, *Soul Retrieval* (San Francisco: HarperSan Francisco, 1991).

9. The Wild Hunt's latest diluted and dumbed-down manifestation is still with us. The Romans, among others, connected the realm of the dead with the idea of wealth: Pluto ruled both. And who rides annually through the sky from the North, drawn by animals and distributing gifts?

10. Pablo Mora, "Día de los muertos plays up the living and the dead," *The Denver Post*, November 2, 1994, 1–F. The writer explains that unlike its family-oriented Mexican prototype, the Colorado celebration had developed partly into self-consciously artistic expressions of political and social satire.

11. Vulcanescu, 270.

12. Robert Gover, *Voodoo Contra* (York Beach, ME: Samuel Weiser, 1985), 77.

13. J. David Lewis-Williams, *Believing and Seeing: Symbolic Meanings in Southern San Rock Paintings* (London: Academic Press, 1981).

14. Gover, 110.

Chapter One

Masks, Religion, & History

Superficially, a priesthood performing a sacred dance while wearing masks and a Passion Play or religious drama are all varieties of the same thing. All around the world, sacred matters are acted out. If there is a difference between the type of masked ritual that this book describes and the religious drama known to the Western world, it is that the masked Witch goes beyond mere "impersonation" or "disguise." To be a Witch, after all, requires a tolerance for ambiguity and for holding more than one idea about the world at once. It means being able to consider the possibility of being one's self and yet, under certain circumstances, someone else.

While masked workings are not modern Witchcraft as most people have come to understand it, the workings may be added to the rites. There is plenty of historical precedent for the practice. We must only remember that any sort of ritual dance is, on one level, an artificial concept based on the knowledge available to us at a given time and expressed through a series of formal movements. We are not saying, therefore, that these workings are essential to the Craft, but that they may be added to it. In some cases, only certain individuals within a coven or group may choose to practice them. They may be worked in conjunction with one of the seasonal Pagan celebrations or on their own—suggestions on how to do this are given in Chapter Seven.

To the extent they have survived, Morris dances, maypole dances, maze dances, ring or circle dances, and all the others have one thing in common. They either serve a magical end—as in the case of the circle dances—or they preserve bits of the Old Faith within them. For instance, a writer named Rhomylly Forbes-Lynx describes her first encounter with masked dancers during a folklore festival in Kentucky this way:

A lone musician suddenly appeared and began to play a recorder. As [if] in response to his haunting melody, six masked dancers in green tabards, each holding a rack of deer antlers to the crown of his head, stepped out from the trees. They wove single file through the trees to the performance area, then formed a small circle that became two lines. The lines advanced toward each other and retreated, each dancer clashing horns with the opposite man, again and again....Eventually they

Abbot's Bromley Horn Dancers, carrying antlers, re-enact a Pagan ritual of the seasons.

This drawing is based on cave art depicting a masked hunter, armed with a bow, pursuing reindeer. Re-enacting the hunt in dance was a way of influencing the gods of the hunt.

reformed into a single file and, again following the musician, wove back through the trees... vanishing into the mist as if they had never been there. I was eight, and though it took me fourteen years to realize it, that night I became a Pagan.[1]

Masked dances like the Morris dances or the Abbots' Bromley Horn Dance re-created as described on the previous page (although the original dance takes place in a village main street) may have begun as Pagan ritual with seasonal significance, before moving into the realm of "folklore." Other masked dances are significant in and of themselves, as in the masked dance of the shaman/priest. All stem from the oldest form of magical working known to humankind, the re-

enactment of an event to influence fortune or the gods of the hunt or for the dancers to contact their guardian spirits or patron deities. In short, the dancers hyped themselves up to a visionary state where they would come face to face with the spirits. Time and constant re-enactment of the concept would lead to a more formal grouping of the dances, making them, in effect, a more specialized magical tool. One dance would be for May Eve, another for Lammas (or whatever seasonal festival a people had), and so on.

Wearing a mask as an aid to moving toward the spirit of an animal or god is then one of the world's oldest magical techniques. For the first hunters, wearing the skin of an animal was not merely functional camouflage, but a way to be psychically "inside" the bear, the bison, or the wolf. Or perhaps it would be more accurate to say Bear, Bison, Wolf—the characters or the archetypes of an entire class of animals—or of the energy that is temporarily personified in the aspect we call a god or god-form. Masking, as noted, is more than impersonation; it makes connections, and at times these connections may last longer than the mere wearing of the mask.

At first, the masked leader of the dance would have been no more than a man dressed up in skins and miming the actions of the hunted animal being tracked down and killed by the hunters. Once again, this act can be seen in cave art with the actual cave gradually becoming the temple to the cult of the animal. Seeing a representation of the animal walking and dancing on two feet would gradually evolve into the concept of the God of the herds in human form and the skin-clad shaman would be the earthly representative of that God.

From this would come the idea of mounting the skull of an animal on a pole and, led by the shaman, dancing around it as an act of worship and thanksgiving for the bodies of the God's brothers that he had sent them to keep them alive. Because of the precarious nature of existence and life, early hunters had to come to terms with the fact that they were part and parcel of the natural order of things; without the herds of game they could not live. They were kindred to the animals, and more and more began to identify with a certain species, becoming the clan of the Bear, Bison, Stag, and so on.

Any encroachment on the hunting grounds of a clan was a threat to the life of the clan. Such a threat could be dealt with only in one way: the intruders either had to be killed or chased off. The dance would be used to hype up the spirits of those doing the actual fighting. In this dance, the spirit of the clan would be invoked to aid the fighters and fill them with courage before the coming scrimmage. In short, the war dance was and still is a form of sacred ritual. For a latter-day parallel, one only has to look at the blessing of the guns or the German Wehrmacht belt buckle stamped with *Gott Mit Uns*, the age-old appeal for their God to be with them.

Eventually the whole concept would become stylized and formal, much in the same way as the Greek tragedies did. When a Greek actor wore the mask of a god in a play, he would pray to the mask and the god to inspire him because he was representing the god while wearing the mask. To render a bad performance was in fact blasphemy against the god and was more than likely to bring down divine disfavor on the actor's head. It took the practical Romans to create a distinct line between what was a sacred play and an act of worship, and what was a bawdy skit. In both cases, masks were used—the Romans developed the comic mask for the comic play and, in effect, secularized the theater.

Throughout history, some combination of masks and dance has been used for worshiping the God and Goddess. Ancient animal-headed masks with holes for straps that attached them to the wearer's head have been found in Egypt. Even earlier were the twenty-five partial stag skulls discovered at the Star Carr archaeological site in Yorkshire. Dating to the Mesolithic Era (Middle Stone Age), the skulls had been cut down, lightened, and drilled, probably for use as parts of a costume. Some historians have suggested they were hunting disguises, which is possible, but a hunter would probably be reluctant to sacrifice agility by tying heavy antlers on his head, whereas a ritual dancer would not have to worry about becoming entangled in brush and branches.

In her controversial books on medieval witchcraft, the British archaeologist Margaret Murray claimed that Inquisitors' reports of "witches dancing before the Devil" in fact depicted worshipers dancing around a masked man who represented the

The Celtic Horned God, Cernunnos, probably derived from the shamanic Herne/Pan spirit of the hunt.

Horned God on earth. "The horns and animal disguise were his 'grand array,' but in his ordinary intercourse with his flock the Incarnate God appeared in the dress of the period. Here again the congregation would see no difference between their own and the Christian priest, who also wore special vestments when performing religious ceremonies."[2] Yet today, apart from the circle dance or "Mill," this way of worshiping seems to have practically disappeared from the occult scene.

We may speculate about how the masked rituals evolved over time, both in their outward and visible forms and in the secret, priestly rites. At the apex of our hypothetical early European tribal mythology would be the Goddess, followed by demigods and demigoddesses and various legendary heroes. All would have animals and birds sacred to them or connected with them. At times, the priests would interpret messages in the behaviors of the various animals and birds.

Most certainly among the Celts there was a tradition of animal and bird reverence as well as a parallel tradition of shape-shifting among the Druid priesthood. Now, unless you wish to accept the concept that a Druid could magically change into a hare, boar, stag, or other animal, there must be another explanation for this shape-shifting. Quite possibly, generations of oral tradition produced a two-tier concept. On the outward level, the priest would claim, "I am a hare, sacred to the Goddess." On an inner level, the reference was to a dream state, an Otherworld in which the physical and psychic blended to become the inspired prophetic world of personal contact between priest and deity.

When the priest, shaman, or Druid claimed he was a hare, stag, cat, boar, and so on, it was not just a case of leaping out of bed one morning and saying

to himself, "Oh, goody goody gumdrops, I think I'll be a hare today." Far from it. By claiming that he had changed to a hare, the priest was saying, "As a man I went to the sacred rite. There I donned the cloak and mask of hare and danced my message to the Goddess. From Her I bring back a reply, for I am Hare and sacred to Her until I become man again and pass on what She has told me to those of Her following."

By going to the rite and putting on the mask and then joining in the circle dance, one particular member had gone into the ecstatic trance-like dance where this world ceased to exist for him and where he met the spirit of the god of the animal whose mask he was wearing. During the dance he would have felt a kinship with the animal, thought of himself as the animal, and in his own mind, become the animal.

The congregation, knowing full well the meaning behind the symbol of the mask, would recognize that the man was no longer a man, but the spirit of the hare talking to his mistress, the goddess of the night. Afterward people would talk about what went on at the meeting and anything that came through—no doubt at the same time talking about old so-and-so who turned into a hare and met the Goddess. Thus the concept of shape-shifting would be born and handed down from generation to generation and with time, losing the explanation of how and why, it became some magical thing that the "old ones" could do—one of the things that the old witches were reputed to be able to do, together with traveling to their meetings by flying on their broomsticks or, having changed into an animal, by running across the open country to the meeting site.

Finally, we can also see how on the visible, outward level, it was possible for masked workings to move out of the realm of magical religion and into the realm of "folklore." We mentioned earlier Morris dancers and such surviving practices as the Abbots' Bromley Horn Dance. These popular masked dances, marked by the appearance of a man dressed as a horse, bull, or other animal, seem to have been connected with the end of the old year and the beginning of the next, a festival that could take place in December, January, or even later. According to E. C. Cawte, an English folklorist who made an extensive study of all the surviving records of Morris dancers, hobby horses (usually a man wearing a draped, horse-shaped framework with an attached horse's head—the wearer's head and torso formed the "rider"), wrote that such dances "largely belong to the winter season....The animals are often killed and revived, or the horses are shod, and thus renewed, both in Great Britain and the rest of Europe."[3]

As many disapproving Christian writers noted, New Year festivals often involved masking with distinct Pagan overtones. Cawte quotes one writer of the fifth century:

> "The new year is consecrated with old blasphemies....Besides, people are dressed as cattle, and men are turned into women....A man is changed into an idol, and if it

Hobby horse dancer at a May Day festival. This dance is more often used to mark the end of the old year and beginning of the new.

© Malcolm Brenner / Eyes Open

is a fault to go to an idol, what can it mean to be one?"[4]

Obviously, the churchman was close to the truth: a masked dancer temporarily manifesting a Pagan deity. Thus, the masked animal dancer concept likely evolved from a far older one, that of the sacrificed Divine Year King. But instead of the sacrifice of the actual living Year King, the ritual became more and more modified until it moved out of the realms of a magical/religious ceremony and into a bit of good old English folklore and custom. By the 1500s, the century of Cawte's oldest written records, hobby horses and Morris dancers had been transformed into church fundraisers, performing at parishioners' homes to raise money for candles, church furnishings, and structural repairs.[5] A blow to their popularity came when the reform-minded king, Edward VI, in 1547 ordered the number of candles used by Anglican churches to be curtailed to a sober few and ordered priests to preach against the custom of burning candles before saints' images. What the Protestant Reformation began, the Puritan triumphs of the English Civil War nearly completed.

Robin Larsen

Morris dancers celebrate the advent of summer with a spirited dance.

The essentially Pagan character of the masked rites reasserts itself to this day. Writing in the 1970s, Cawte notes:

> Anyone who seeks to find an origin in these customs in common human characteristics, so that they could arise by parallel evolution in various unconnected districts, will be interested in a performance of a souling play in a Cheshire Approved School. The boys found the play much easier to learn and perform than others they were given ... and the Wild Horse seemed to know, without rehearsal, exactly what he was supposed to do.[6]

In England today, at Hastings, for example, there is a revival of the Morris dance to release "Jack-in-the-green," but the season has shifted to another turning point of the year, May Day or Beltane. The man playing Jack, a dancing bush which is supposed to harbor the spirit of summer, first dances its way through the town to the castle grounds where it is pushed over to kill it and release the spirit of summer.

Now, if this is looked at as a religious rite and not just another piece of English folklore, then a recognizable pattern emerges. The rite itself would not have started on the morning of May Day, but on May Eve. The members of the coven would have gathered at mid-

Robin Larsen, mask made by Lauren Raine

This mask might be worn by dancer portraying the Green Man.

night and celebrated their rites where at an earlier date, the sacrificial victim would have been made ready for the sunrise sacrifice. In later times, the selected dancer would have been masked and cloaked in greenery and then, invoking the spirit of summer to enter him, would at sunrise lead off in a dance that would take him around and then through the settlement to the place where he would be "killed" in a symbolic manner. He would slip out of the disguise after being pushed over and leave it where it lay; thus the people would see a now-dead bush and realize that in a sympathetic magical way, the spirit of summer was now free to spread across the land. They would of course have known that the bush was a disguised man; they would have also known that nobody was actually killed and would have realized that what they had witnessed was a sacred drama re-enacting a magical spell—once again, a theatrical and magical drama with the masked dancer at its core.

Undoubtedly there would have been some form of dance for all the major festivals. But like so many of the ancient ways, only a handful of them survive, mainly because of their importance to the populace. Of them all, May Eve and the Christmas/New Year period seem to be the most popular survivals. As another example of Pagan survival, one only has to look at the Abbots' Bromley horn dance. These famous horns have for centuries been housed in the Church but only on the understanding that the horns belong to the people and the dance is done for the people.

Theories on the origins of the dance are many and varied, but no one can say for sure just how old it is. Certain facts serve as a pointer to its ancient and Pagan past. The costumes of the dancers are Victorian in origin; before that, dancers wore their ordinary clothes decorated with ribbons. Most certainly, the inclusion of the hobby horse and Maid Marian are a later addition that brings this performance into line with the traditional Morris dance. Also, the wooden heads that the horns

are mounted on are far younger than the horns themselves.

One other point of interest is the date of performing the dance: it does not correspond with any of the four major rituals. It used to be traditional for the dancers to hold an overnight vigil on St. Bartholomew's Eve (August 23) before taking the horns out for the dance. The church where the horns are held is dedicated to St. Nicholas, a favored dedication when a church was built on what was once a Pagan site.

In summary, we are looking at dance with all the trappings of a hunting culture ritual for the good of a certain community. Christianized though it was, at one time the horn dance would have been preceded by another ritual on the eve of the dance. To legitimize the concept and make it acceptable to a Christian community, this rite became an all-night vigil in the parish church. One other thing to be noted is that the actual dance starts off as a circle dance before changing its character. Could this be a memory of an old coven gathering by the priest/dancers on the eve of a public performance, a gathering of what today would be called a coven of witches?

Another surviving dance, although not presently connected with masking, is the maze dance, often called "Troytown" in Britain. Of all the religious forms of dance, the maze dance is the least understood. In fact, no one can be quite sure that the maze dance was a dance in the accepted meaning of the word. In the past, walking or running the maze was part and parcel of the old countryside celebratory ways that have now passed into the realms of folklore and custom—in other words, "something the English used to do way back." Perhaps because the maze dance has lasted for as long as it has, the theory and concept behind it have changed or been modified to suit the times and changes of opinion that it was set in. Certainly in Europe the maze as a religiously significant pattern survives from the pre-Christian Bronze Age right through to the building of the great medieval cathedrals. In both Spain and France the maze pattern was used in the floor decoration of some cathedrals, and one of the finest preserved examples is to be found in Chartres Cathedral. The strange thing is that you will never find maze-patterned flooring in England that is as old as the Continental mazes. Even though in Britain there are mazes connected with churches, they follow the peculiarly British habit of being turf-cut rather than the Continental style of laying the internal paths in tile or mosaic and the external ones in stone.

Modern-day Pagans tred a maze just as their predecessors did during the Bronze Age.

Historically speaking, the maze concept must have been a fairly universal one as examples have been found as far apart as Iceland, Sweden, and other Scandinavian countries, as well as throughout northern Europe and the Mediterranean. Perhaps in the naming of them there is some clue to their origin. "Troytown," or "the walls of Troy" are among the names given to them and may indicate a Grecian origin. The most famous and most well-documented maze was the Cretan labyrinth, home of the Minotaur, the half-man, half-bull creature often interpreted has having been a bull-masked priest or sacrificial victim. In the story that comes down to us from ancient Athens, the Minotaur is reputed to have killed all who came against him until he too was killed by Theseus, an Athenian prince who thus freed his city from an annual sacrificial tribute. One thing is certain: the labyrinth maze of Crete had an important significance, established by the fact that it became part of the decoration found on Cretan coins. Ariadne, the Cretan princess who aided Theseus, may represent a goddess herself; her name means "holy one."

Whatever the maze's origins, we can say with certainty that, like Maypole dancing, Morris dancing, well dressing, and other popular practices, maze treading became part of the country scene and one of the games played as part of the summertime festivals or holidays, until it died away under the twin onslaughts of the Protestant Reformation and the Industrial Revolution. People who have trodden the maze very often recognize that locked within the twisting, turning pathway there is a force, power, or energy that is felt by the dancer, and furthermore, this power feels like a friendly if neglected one. Perhaps it is nothing more than the residue of the power and knowledge sought by the dancers of a bygone age and only found within the twistings and turnings of the mystic maze. This raises one more question: is the maze a pattern laid out on one of the "hot spots" of a sacred site, or does the maze through its twistings and turnings create the power within itself? One possible answer to this question will be offered later in the book.

Let us then examine these different strands as part of a whole. A Pagan form of shamanistic religious dance still exists. It can take two forms, one magical and one semi-secular. The magical form of dance is the circle dance, or as it is sometimes known, "treading the Mill." This in turn has two forms: widdershins (counterclockwise) for serious or magical workings, and deosil (clockwise), a celebratory, lighthearted dance for sheer enjoyment. A Pagan religious rite is danced out, usually by some form of disguised dancer as a public display of the rite being done in a symbolic and meaningful way.

More than a few traces of this are hidden in the Morris dances and horn dances similar to the Abbots' Bromley Horn dance. Changed out of all recognition and with later additions like Robin Hood, Maid Marian, the Doctor, the Jester, and so on, the dances still have within them a fair amount of the old lore—and deep down, people still respond to the magic of them. The other form of dance is the maze dance, of whose origins little is known, but perhaps there is more than a strong memory of it enshrined in the Witches'

spiral dance. A spiral dance in effect is a simplified maze dance that could be done in secret without a formally laid-out maze path.

Dances such as the Abbots' Bromley horn dance, the traditional Morris dance, "Jack in the Green," or their equivalents in other countries enshrine another aspect of the Old Religion, one not practiced much by the modern Witch. Nevertheless, it is an important aspect because through these old dances runs a strong element of the Old Faith, even though they are nowadays performed out of context. (And that is how they will stay unless more covens take up Morris dancing! Best of luck to them, for this form can be hard going.)

Horn dancers and musicians at Abbots' Bromley.

Like all mystery traditions, the Old Religion was a two-tiered system—worshipers and initiates. "Initiate" means the priest, the rest of the population were the worshipers and, as such, would have understood the public or openly performed rites as well as taking part in them.

Take May Day as an example: on May Eve you would have celebrated the priestly or coven rites dedicated to the Goddess, Queen of the heavens and the night. Once these were done, the next sunrise would herald the dawning of May Day and the public

May Pole dancers wind their way around the traditional pole.

© Malcolm Brenner / Eyes Open

rites would be performed, re-enacting in a symbolic way the drama of the Divine King's sacrifice. This sacrifice would have actually taken place the night before. The part of the rite linking the two events together would be when the priest sprinkled the waiting crowd as a blessing with the blood of the sacrificed Divine King mixed with water, after which parts of the king's body would have been buried in various fields along with other rites including copulation between a priest and priestess.

Of course, time would modify the concept of the two forms of worship and rites, and to a certain degree change them, but the basic concept of those two forms of worship and ritual would not have been modified. With the enlargement of the group or clan to a tribal one, within an enlarged tribal area, the rites would have become more and more centralized and focused on one sacred place that would eventually become the tribal sacred site. Scattered communities would gather for these rites and feast, dance, and shake off the hardships of the past winter season as well as welcome the coming spring. These sacred areas would not only be a sacred place for the tribal rites but a place where people met, exchanged goods and news, found spouses, and settled debts and disputes, until gradually the site would become the recognizable forerunner of the four great seasonal meeting places or fairs. In the same way, the coven priesthood would become more and more interlinked with each other rather than just being a few people serving a group or clan and dancing the sacred dances in isolation for that group alone.

Maze magic remains difficult to reconstruct. We know that once people danced them and that they are significant in a religious sense, and that their significance spanned a long period of time. Under Christianity, the spiral twisting path that led to the innermost heart of the maze was called the "Path to Jerusalem," "The City of God," or "The Place of Christ's Passion." By identifying the maze with Christ, people of those times apparently Christianized a long-familiar and long-treasured Pagan mythos of the death and resurrection cycle: the journey taken to the underworld through the spiral of existence.

One Witches' dance—the spiral dance—bears a strong resemblance to the maze dance. Our tradition has it that this dance represents the journey to the Spiral Castle wherein would be found the Cauldron of Inspiration, presided over by the Pale-Faced Goddess herself, and guarded by nine maidens. Also, this hall was the dwelling-place of the shades of long-dead heroes and the demigods of the old tradition. Within the Witches' spiral dance, the old knowledge and meaning still held true to what it had always stood for. Even though it is not practiced widely today, it is still a valid a working tool, just as it was in the past. Because its magic can never be lost or destroyed, only neglected, more modern Witches need to take new looks at the concept, creating new forms of maze or spiral dances as an expression of their own beliefs, while at the same time re-awakening the old magic held within the spiral way.

For some Witches, the spiral or maze dances display the magic of illusion, for in the creation of the illusion, we realize that on the surface of the rite there is one effect, while on another level, there is an inward feeling of inspiration and understanding—illusion and reality coming together to create inspiration. One "script" for this dance will be given in Chapter Six, in which the coveners begin by dancing the circle and then are led by the masked figure of Raven out of the circle and into a spiral dance leading toward a marked center, then out again and back to the circle.

Notes

1. Rhomylly Forbes-Lynx, "Beyond the Maypole," *Enchanté* 13 (Divali/Yule, 1992) 7–8.

2. Margaret A. Murray, *The God of the Witches* (London: Oxford University Press, 1970 [1931]), 35.

3. E. C. Cawte, *Ritual Animal Disguise* (Cambridge: D. S. Brewer, Ltd., 1978), p. 224.

4. Cawte, 225.

5. Cawte, Chapter 2, *passim*. Ironically, the first known appearance of the English term, "hobby horse," is in a Welsh-language poem from the late 1300s.

6. Cawte, 226.

Chapter Two

The Dance as a Magical Tool

Both Eastern and Western occult traditions recognize the importance of some sort of breathing control in any meditation or magical working rite. The concept behind this is to divorce the body from the soul or spirit and the spirit from this world. The sacred dance does much the same thing, be it the rapid circular gyrations of the shaman/priest seeking to reach his own spirit-guardian through the ecstatic dance and the resultant shortage of breath, or the slow, circular pacing of the "Mill" with its long, drawn-out circle chant. Each of these has the same end in mind, the disorientation of the body to a greater or lesser degree, and with this disorienting, the opening up of the mind to the gods or the Goddess—call it what you will: "bringing about a group ecstasy," "creating mental tension" or the many other names used to try and explain it. One thing is sure, there is no getting away from the basic fact that people do experience this sort of trance or trance-like dance, and do feel they have had contact with their guiding spirit or god, or even the Goddess Herself.

In the slowly trodden "Mill," the slow dance or pacing of the circle, the aim is to raise power in a form that can be manipulated or directed toward a given end. The same form of breathing control is used, but the dancers doing the Mill create within their minds a rhythmic drum-like beat with the words "EEEEEE... AAAAAA...IIIIII...OOOOO" in a drawn-out, monotonous, repetitive chant. Gradually the mind empties itself of all that is going on around it. Nothing exists but the circle, the chant, and the pace. One has the illusion of being in the center of a large black nothing that is constantly moving in waves or pulses. For a while, the waves seem to roll in toward the center of this black universe, and all the time there is this feeling of pressure slowly building up and then a sudden giving way. From that moment on, the waves of darkness roll outwards and with this rolling outwards, the power is raised within the circle by the treading of the mill, raising the magic of the working rite.

When the coveners "Tread the Mill" for magical purposes, the movement is counter-clockwise or widdershins. When they move faster, clockwise or deosil, the aim is release. The deosil dance is used after a ceremonial act of worship; widdershins is the proper direction for a working rite with a serious magical intent. Later, having partaken of the cakes and wine, the last part of the Witches' rite would be the deosil or sun-wise dance.

Having done this on more than one occasion, I can only say how it affects me. Starting off slowly, the dance seems to gradually pick up speed. As the pace grows faster, a euphoric burst of high spirits and laughter seems to spontaneously bubble up from deep inside. Though this is not of deep magical significance in itself, it is a magical thing because everything seems to drop away. All the cares and worries, the unpleasantness of the world, disappears in a burst of laughter. At the feast afterward, people let their hair down and enjoy themselves. I remember how after one meeting some of the coven members were having great fun chasing little blue lights in and out of the bushes and laughing uproariously.

Another occasion when something like this occurred was at a Candlemas meeting. After we had finished working and were leaving the site, we began spontaneously to re-enact the old Wild Hunt, horn-blowing and all. We literally ran through the woods to the road. After we stopped, one member of the party drew our attention to what we had done; we had run the Wild Hunt. All I can say is that this was something that seized us all, picked us up and made us run through the woods, leaving us at the end breathless and glad to be alive. Also, I am willing to wager that more than one person who heard us cowered under the bedclothes wondering what was going on. For a while we had reached the stage where we did not care what could be heard by others—we were all lost in the spirit of the dance or cross-country gallop, conscious of our surroundings yet at the same time not part of them.

Consciously, we had not wanted noise and excitement at all—quite the opposite. Tradition may have it that the old Wild Hunt used to end in this way, but at the time the last thing we wanted was a couple of policemen with their "Hello, hello, and what's all this then?" In spite of all our feeling, an atavistic spirit had taken over, making us do as our ancestors once had done.

In both forms of circle dance, the technique is the same, even though the ends differ. Breathing control coupled with the circular motion introduces the feeling of disorientation. At a certain stage, the mind becomes receptive to the external and psychic influences; thus the link is made between the Gods and the worshiper, and even though the rite is wound down, sometimes the aftermath can still be in the hands of the old Horned God.

Within mainstream religion—which for Europe and North America means Christianity—trance-inducing dance has long been frowned upon. In the eighteenth century, John Wesley and other evangelical reformers were looked at askance because their followers were finding God too quickly for their own good and with too much enthusiasm—which originally meant "being filled with [a] god." Today, little has changed. Certain fringe denominations have developed a trance-like rite of "possession by the Holy Spirit," but they have never been fully accepted by the more orthodox churches, mainly on the grounds that their practices border on heresy, recalling some

Jeff Farnam

Native Americans use the circle form for their dances, and drums set the pace.

of the heretical Gnostic sects of early Christianity.

As for what are now known as the "ethnic faiths," they were simply beyond the pale and about on a par with non-classical Paganism. Yet it is among the so-called fringe faiths and ethnic religion that the concept of finding God, or the Gods, Goddesses, and Guardian Spirits, through the medium of trance-inducing dances is not only understood but used to bring about a greater understanding of the relationship between the individual and his or her God or Goddess.

Most certainly the technique of the dance is known to the followers of Voodoo; similarly, fringe Christian groups use a kindred form of ecstasy during their gatherings when they handle poisonous snakes, or to bring about conversion and the opening up to God. In all these cases, the art lies in the creation of an artificial stimulus to bring about both mental and physical changes in the body as a way of opening up the mind to God or the Gods.

What we as Witches may understand better than some, however, is that not everyone is suited to this form of worship—plus the fact that in many other cults, the aims and aspirations are very different than those aimed at during a Witch dance. Those other groups may intend to involve the congregation in the rites while the leaders,

in effect, stand back and control the workings. In the Witch dance, with its deliberate aim, those involved in this form of dance-worship would be coven members of long standing. Furthermore, there would never be non-initiates present or taking part in the rite. The dance is for the experienced only and should never impinge on normal coven workings, remaining as a separate set of rites that extend and amplify the workings within the main body of the worship.

Coupled with the trance-like inspirational dance brought about by controlled breathing and bodily changes is the wearing of the sacred mask. In some ways it is the mask that chiefly creates the magic of illusion. Just as there will be physical changes in the body when the dance is being done, when the mask is donned, there should be mental changes as well. It is the change in mental attitudes that is one of the hardest things to bring about because, in effect, you have to cease being yourself. In some ways it is like rubbing the hand down over the face to remove the make-up that is the face you present to the world—an easy thing to say but a very hard thing to do. To create the illusion of inwardly being something else, one first has to have the knowledge and then the understanding of the entity being portrayed, much in the same way that actors have to learn their lines and then express the characters they are playing.

Make no mistake; as a masked dancer, you are playing a role. When wearing the mask, you have to interpret that character within the formal framework of the mythos as understood by the coven and represented by the mask that you are wearing. During the dance or pacing, on one level you know who you are as opposed to what you are representing; then gradually the persona of the mask begins to come to the fore. You as a person recede into the background of your consciousness while the illusion of the mask becomes the reality within the dance. It is while in this state of reality that you come face to face with the God or Goddess of the mask that you are wearing. For this particular meeting, you become the messenger of the Gods and the soul within the mask as well as an extension of the Godhead itself.

Some other religious traditions aim to bring the participants to an ecstatic state; in ours, individuals bring themselves to the same state but in a more controlled manner. The aim is deliberate, the intention deliberate, with all of this being directed to one end: to bring one dancer to the fore as the leader of the dance. This person will be the visionary dancer of the meeting. The others, though masked and participat-

Karen St. Pierre

The Green Man is a key performer in the masked dances.

ing, will not reach the same ecstatic state because they serve as the control for the whole of the rite that is being done. They are the ones to help the dancer over and then back to this world. In this sort of ritual there is room for one visionary and one visionary only. To try and push others over the border at the same time can only lead to chaos and danger to both the group and the individual.

Like all things of a spiritual or magical nature, there is always that little seed of doubt concerning what has happened: is it genuine phenomena or is it something more in line with wishful thinking, even though it may be on a subconscious level and unintentional or not as the case may be? One thing is sure, as any experienced ritualist will tell you, there must always be a healthy air of skepticism about any acceptance of phenomena. This is where training comes in. On both the individual and the group or coven level, the well-integrated gathering works toward a recognizable and desired end through knowledge, understanding, and above all, practice in the techniques of the concept. To accept this, one must accept the fact that the dance is a long-established magical tool in all its forms. The mask likewise is a tool for creating a magical impression on both an outward as well as an inward level. By donning one, you say, "I present a face of divinity to the world." On an inward plane, you say, "With the wearing of this mask, I take on the attributes of (whatever form the mask represents) and through this, I become the mouthpiece and servant of the God or Goddess. May I be filled with the wisdom of the yet-unspoken word and that the understanding that is inherent in life be granted to me."

Finally, and perhaps the most important question of all, who are these animals and birds? Why have they been sacred and why these specific ones among thousands of others? In the following pages, these questions are answered and all the separate strands that go together to make a cohesive whole are drawn together, creating what, for want of a better name, are called the "Masked Rites of Tubal Cain."

Chapter Three

Animals and Birds Sacred to the Rites

The Following of Tubal Cain have adopted the thirteen animals or birds mentioned below for the masked dance rites of the clan.[1] Coven members, always thirteen in number, may each represent a different entity. They are Stag, Raven, Squirrel, Owl, Fox, Boar, Goose, Cat, Ram, Hare, Mare, Hound, Swan.

Arbitrary as this selection may seem, it is based on historical and recorded coven practices in the British Isles. This is not to say that any or all of these could be left out of the list, or that any group could not select a different set of animals and birds. (For suggestions on how to do this, see Chapter Seven.) Remember, however, that any animal or bird chosen should have a traditional connection with the Gods and with the rites. Let us now look at them in turn to determine how and why they were chosen.

These creatures stretched across differing cultures and time spans, sometimes changing in emphasis, or taking on other aspects, or losing certain aspects within the body of Pagan myths that became the common heritage of the European races. Diverse European beliefs gathered from Celtic, Germanic, and Scandinavian sources formed the basis of the faith that later became the pre-Christian matter of Anglo-Saxon England.

The Mask of Stag

Of all the masks, perhaps Stag is the oldest, stretching back to the earliest shaman-priest of the cave paintings. Priest to the God of the herds, the shaman would have been robed in deer hide, wearing the antlers of a stag as part of the rite. He would have danced the dance of the stalking and then the killing of the game animal as a form of sympathetic magical aid to the hunters of the group. The same Horned God figure was still to be found among pastoral cultures, but instead of being the God of the hunt, He became the God of the herds and the God of fertility of the herds. To the Celts, he was the God Cernunnos, and in a blending of Celtic and Anglo-Saxon mythology, a concept emerges and crystallizes into a formal mythos of the Stag-King dancer and leader of the group, shaping the ritual actions of the priest/dancer and servant of the Gods.

In the "Song of Amergin," attributed to a legendary Druidic poet, occurs the line, "I am a stag of seven tines," or, sometimes, "I am a stag of seven fights." Looked at in another way, this line could be saying, "I am the king of the seven-year reign." Couple this with the image of the "roebuck in the thicket," and we have the concept of a Divine King sacrificed (if only metaphorically) within the confines of a sacred grove to allow the new seven-year king to reign.

In our Craft tradition, we see a stag-masked leader paying a ceremonial death price at the end of a seven-year rule. This death would have been a symbolic one with a blood sacrifice as a substitute for the leader's own death, and with a renewal of the pledge to the Gods and the oath of leadership. The stag-masked leader of the dance, after being leader for seven years, would undergo a symbolic and ritual death on the horns of the God before being reborn again and pledging to lead the dancers in his newly born spirit guise as Stag, king of the dance.

The thicket where the stag is held is pictured symbolically not so much as a clump of tangled saplings, but rather as a solitary tree: the World Tree Yggdrasill, the mighty ash, the tree that forms the bridge between the Underworld, the physical world we inhabit, and the world of the heavens. In this light, the ash pole of the stang represents not only the God but the ash tree of life as well.

In the story of the hanging of Odin on the sacred Ash, there is a twofold concept. One is the sacrifice by hanging to the God, paralleling the symbol of the roebuck in the thicket trapped by its horns, or King Stag trapped and hung by his horns from the sacred tree. As well as the obvious sacrificial element in this, there is also a magical one. The concept of suffering upon the sacred tree as part of the initiation of a shaman/priest crops up in many unrelated cultures. By undergoing a symbolic ritual dream-state death, the shaman gains secret and esoteric knowledge while in a visionary state. Part of the knowledge is the ability of shape-shifting.

This ability has been described as sending the spirit out in animal or bird form, much the same way as Odin used to send out his two ravens, Thought

and Memory. In ecstatic dance state, the statement "I am what I claim to be, and I can both see and hear, so therefore I remember" sums up rather neatly what the dance is all about. The persistence of shamanistic elements in the worship of Odin and a continuity of beliefs between the Dark Age Saxon and the later Vikings suggests how the concept could pass down through the ages to be echoed later as an aspect of Anglo-Saxon or English Witchcraft.

Stag leads the dance, carrying the horned wand or staff, which he then passes on to another dancer at the start of the rite. This staff then is passed from hand to hand around the circle until someone feels the urge to claim it and hold it for the duration of the dance. Stag then breaks the circle and

Chas S. Clifton, mask made by Martin Anthony

The stag-masked dancer leads the sacred dance.

takes a place well away from the rest of the dancers. Although still the leader of the dance in one sense, he also becomes the dual symbol of Stag leader and King of the Castle or the King within the Castle, the "castle" in this case being the castle/mound of the grave. This "castle" is the place entered by the shaman/priest to gain the knowledge of past, present, and future. His is the spirit who guides the shaman through the labyrinth to the cauldron—or, looking at it another way, the one who guides the priest leader of the dance through death and into the Underworld and then back again while the priest is in animal guise.

Back in this world once again, the priest or priestess of the dance gradually slips back into human spiritual form, losing the eyes of the animistic spirit he or she invoked to see beyond the boundaries of this world.

The final part of the ritual dance is the homage paid to King Stag as the dancers slowly dance around him in a circle and pass the horned wand from hand to hand through the ranks until it reaches him. He comes down from the mound no longer King of the Castle, for he has reverted back to King Stag, leader of the dance once again.

In spite of the recognition of the stag and its mythos and symbology, we must keep in mind that it is difficult to define its exact role within the rites.

The stag as such can represent the Herne-Cernunnos God figure of the animals, the tribal totem head, and so on. One only has to look at the little statuette of the red deer stag (which would be similar to a North American bull elk) on display in the Brighton museum to see that here is something special. Attributed to the first or second centuries of the present era, the little piece of bronze has been tentatively described as a temple cult object of some Sussex-dwelling Romano-Celtic following. Unproveable, yes, but looked at in the light of the stag-masked, hide-covered magician/shaman of cave-painting fame, then tied into the mythos of the horned hunter (an example of which is reputed to haunt the great oak in Windsor Great Park), there is a consistency in the recognition of the stag being in some ways set apart from other horned animals.

Other cultures would look to other horned animals as being the symbol of the Deity: the goat-foot Pan figure of Greek and Roman classical mythology, the white bull sacrifice of the Persian Mithraic cult that later played an important part in the religious climate of the late Roman Empire. All these in their own way recognized a living animistic representation of the Godhead as well as the relationship between humans and their God.

As an illustration of this, one only has to look at one of the finds from a dig in what was once Ur in present-day Israel. This was a model of a ram-within-the-thicket and it is more than possible that in ancient Ur there was a parallel development of the concept we know as the Roebuck within the thicket, with the wild ram taking the place of the Roebuck within the mythos. In most people's eyes, unproveable, yes, but at the same time, possible—at least, I like to think so.

Even today, high in the Austrian Alps where the chamois still lives and is still hunted, when the hunter makes his kill and the body of the animal is being brought down the mountain, both the guides and the local villagers make a great thing of photographing and recording the kill. This is not done so much for the benefit of the hunter, but to honor the quarry. As part of these rites, a juniper twig dipped in the blood of the kill is worn in the hunter's hat, along with a tuft of long hair clipped from the underbelly of the chamois. The second twig is placed in the mouth of the animal with the serious magical intent of linking both the hunter and the quarry together, while at the same time ensuring that the spirit of the animal will not come back to trouble the man who killed it. Christian the people may be, but in this custom is the long-held memory

that the chamois is different and set apart from other horned animals. It was once suspected of having the power to come back in spirit form to haunt the slayer, much in the same way as the stag was once regarded in this country. There is still a certain mystique in the killing of a deer with a much-prized "trophy" head.

To fully understand the role of stag—or its equivalent—within the rites and the dance, one must first understand the nature of the stag himself, following his life through the year-long cycle. The young stags challenge him at rutting time, and the year comes when age has slowed and weakened him and he is chased away from the does. Likewise, you must begin to feel and understand the young stag bellowing his challenge to the old leader and losing until he is strong enough to win that supremacy. By understanding this, you begin to understand the nature of the stag; in an esoteric way, there is a blending of stag as the animal and stag as a symbol and mystic concept. Doing this, build up your own group or coven lore, the feeling and understanding of what the stag-within-the-rites will mean to you, how the group will visualize and interpret the mask of stag in a way that is personal to both you and yours so that in the end, you have a spirit of stag as you see and understand him to be.

Make no mistake, the "old ones" did not evolve their religious concepts and faith through reading great and learned tomes; far from it, they found it through observation, seeing and remembering what was going on around them. Seeing with an understanding eye, they found something that linked them into the ebb and flow of nature, making them part of that cycle and with this, a certain understanding. Coupled with this understanding was a yearning or longing to give form to a realized but undefined Spirit of Creation that nowadays we call the Gods or the Goddess, or maybe, just God. In some ways perhaps we are lucky: we can see with the same sort of eyes they did, we can understand with the same sort of understanding as they had and at the same time, shape this understanding to suit our own needs and aspirations as well as our own unfulfilled longings instead of being tied to their traditions. In this sense, the rites of the mask and dance should be looked upon as the start of a voyage of exploration and discovery, searching out or rediscovering the old truths and adapting them to suit the present day.

The Mask of Raven

Imagine corpses on a northern battle-field. Scavenging ravens would have been a common sight there when the dead and wounded might lie for days before being carried away, if ever they were. The image of a raven landing on the body of a dead or wounded man would lead to the conclusion that when the bird flew off, it carried with it the dead warrior's soul. Hence the personification of the Morrigan, the Celtic war goddess, dangerous and deceitful, selecting those who are about to die, marking them for their coming deaths, and carrying them off to her castle. In the ritual dance, likewise, Raven takes the dancers to the Underworld so that their spirits may partake of the bounty of the Cauldron of Inspiration and Knowledge before returning to this world. (As a point of interest, the Irish Druid Mog Ruith at the siege of Druim

Damnggair called for his hide of the hornless dun bull and his *enchennach* or bird dress before working his magic against the defenders. His actions were a recognizable form of ritualistic shape-shifting before a magical working.)

This connection with death, souls, and the Underworld gives this "ill-omened" bird an important place within the ritual of the mask and dance. Perhaps one of the most potent pieces of magic that I have ever witnessed was the chant of the Raven dancer during a cursing: in a way, it sums up rather neatly one aspect of the Raven figure as a ritual being within the group.

I am Raven
haunter of the field of battle
messenger of the Pale-Faced
Goddess my Mistress
By earth...by air...by fire...by
water

29

and under the moon, the
symbol of our Goddess.
I claim that the horns of
the God
are stained with the blood of
sacrifice
that has yet to be taken.
For you are that sacrifice that
has yet to die.
Thus your blood is dedicated
to the Horned God and your
body
to the carrion eaters.
The flames of the fires of
purification
shall sear your flesh from the
living bone
and burn out the evil that is
within you.
Agony and damnation shall
claim your living soul
and my talons shall pierce
your still-beating heart.
Madness and terror shall walk
hand in hand with you
as you stand accursed for all
eternity.
For I am Raven and you shall
learn to fear me
for I am the eater of death
and messenger
to the dark side of the Goddess.
Accursed are you,
and accursed you shall be,
for you are the essence
of what we see as evil,
and the evil that is within you
shall surely die along with
your very soul itself.
So I have spoken, so shall it
be done.

But Raven is more than the personification of dark vengeance. Even though from this side of death Raven may be seen to be an ill-omened bird bearing away the souls of the newly dead, at the same time, we must remember that the dead soul goes to the place of rest and forgetfulness, awaiting the time of rebirth. It is in this context that the Raven dancers fill their role within the rites. Raven leads off the dance that treads the spiral path to the center of the maze, then leads the dancers out again. In the same sense, the spiral path is symbolic of the spiral of life; the dancers tread it to the center that represents the castle/grave mound presided over by the Horned God/Stag King. By doing this, each dancer in effect mimics a pseudo-death, only to be reborn again after absorbing the lessons or secrets that are only to be found in the place beyond the grave. When re-treading the path back to the outside again, one is creating the symbolic rebirth back into this world.

A second piece of Raven's persona comes from the Nordic past: the twin ravens of Odin, mentioned above, who were named Thought and Memory. When we tread the spiral path, even though in a symbolic way, we hope to recall the hidden memories from past lives that are locked up in the entity we call the soul. This shamanistic concept is still useful

Mask and photo by Robin Larson

Raven leads the dancers to the "castle."

today because not only are we tapping into the internal memories and powers, we are also tapping into the external forces that are all around us, even though they are hidden within the fabric of life and nature of the very world we were born into.

Raven carries the wand or staff of office when the group or coven sets out to tread the spiral way as a ritual. King Stag, symbol of the Horned God, would pass the staff to Raven, indicating that Raven is now the messenger of the Goddess. Raven now leads the group first into the "Mill" pacing dance. When instinct tells Raven that the time is right, the group shifts into the spiral or maze dance. Be it the simple Witches' spiral dance or the more

complicated formal maze dance, the aim of the dance remains the same: to disorient the body and the mind from this world, leaving the inner self or spirit free to make the crossing between the world of the physical and the world of the psychic.

One must create the image of this journey within the subconscious by creating a series of landmarks that lead to the center or the core of reality that is expressed as the Castle and the Hall, wherein is found the cauldron presided over by the Pale-Faced Goddess Herself. Raven leads the souls of the dancers to Her sacred halls where they await the giving of knowledge to them by the Goddess.

Well-performed, Raven's dance offers the feeling and the knowledge that there is another entity, power, or force responding to the rite while at the same time remaining part of the maze or spiral path. At the same time, there is an underlying feeling of remoteness, timelessness, and age that seems to span time, place, and distance, and with this, realization that the concept of the God and the Goddess is far bigger than anyone could possibly imagine, encompassing all of creation, life, nature, and finally death in past, present, and future. The whole concept is endlessly repeating itself over and over again and you, as part of this cycle, are locked into it until the spark of divinity that is called the soul is ready to be reunited with the God-head from whence it came.

Raven-the-dancer is a concept or symbol, and as such has transcended many cultures. In the case of modern masked dance rites, there must be a cross-fertilizing of both old and new ideas, with the aims, aspirations, and ends toward which you as a group are working. Above all, the things brought back from the circle and the maze are the ones that not only shape the future workings but also help you to understand something of yourself, something of the meaning of life and what life can be for you as an individual. So the twin ravens of "Thought and Memory" hold out the keys to the future and where present and future can to some extent be shaped to form the past that has yet to come.

In addition, Raven is the trickster—trickster in the sense that Raven must create the illusion that is an integral part of the Raven dance, creating within each of the dancers the mental imagery of the pathway to the center of the maze. As well as treading the actual physical maze or path, one must also tread the mythical maze path within the mind. It is this path that is seen with the inner eye that leads to the cas-tle, and within the castle to the hall of the Goddess.

In one sense, Raven must create something out of nothing and give it a recognizable form so that the journey along the maze or spiral path is a jour-ney of enchantment. In the mind's eye, the path becomes a tree-fringed track, twisting and turning back on itself, gradually leading to the glade wherein lies the castle. Leading the gathering is raven, not the raven/man figure of real-ity, but the bird itself, flying from branch to branch, leading the party deeper and deeper into the woods.

To fully understand this, it must be realized that the illusion will take on a certain air of reality with time, even though this reality will be of the mind. Part of the duties of Raven will be to create this atmosphere, weaving a spell of words and word pictures and every-one present must allow this atmosphere to take possession of them until they begin to live and experience it as fact rather than illusion. Yet above all, we must still recognize the illusion for what it is, and, at the same time, still be able to draw a measure of under-standing from it. For it is in this dream vision state that you will meet the Goddess you have chosen to worship of your own free will, face to face.

The Mask of Squirrel

Squirrel is the shaman of the group, shaman in the sense of being a trance-medium, not in the passive sense of holding hands around a table top and then going into a trance but more in the way of the old idea of first finding the spirit aspect or guardian-spirit-form that will become personal to the shaman or Squirrel dancer and to them alone.

To dance the part of Squirrel, a Witch must train in how to go into a trance at will, taking with him or her the questions that are to be asked of the guardian spirit of the group. Separating the soul from the body in a trance state, the soul then shape-shifts into the form of a small animal. From the European viewpoint, the squirrel's shamanic role has always been connected with the World Tree Yggdrasill that stretches from its roots in the

Underworld through to this world, with its upper branches in the heavens. Squirrel as a tree dweller moves freely up and down the tree. In a trance-state, the squirrel/medium is able to act as the messenger between the three worlds by using the World Tree as a ladder. From the middle of the trunk that symbolizes our world, he or she is able through trance-state to visit both the Underworld and the heavens.

In its natural habitat, the squirrel builds up a store of nuts and berries to see it through the winter. Walking through the woods in the late autumn, one can often find an odd nut or acorn dropped by a squirrel. Once I saw a gray squirrel drop an acorn, which I took home and planted. I now have a three-inch oak growing in the garden. Symbolically, the nut contains knowl-edge: in Celtic mythology, it is eaten

33

by the salmon. Squirrel, by its powers while in a trance state, is able to move freely between the three worlds or the three states of existence and is able to retain knowledge gained from this and memorize it. In effect, this store of knowledge is analogous to the store of nuts hoarded by the squirrel. Each little bit of knowledge passed out by the Squirrel dancer contains within it a kernel of what we consider to be the ultimate truth.

Rooted in a shamanistic past, Squirrel's role in some ways resembles the Nordic cult of the Vanir, the older gods of that pantheon. There is a specific connection between the Goddess Freya and a certain type of Witchcraft called *seithr*; indeed, the Goddess Freya, according to the saga writer Snorri, was a priestess of the Vanir cult.

Enough is known about seidr magic to see how the priestess/practitioner of the rites would in many ways act as pointer to the role of the squirrel dancer. Before the rite, a tall wooden platform would be erected where the *volva* or priestess/seer would be seated. The rite included singing and chanting spells used to bring about a state of ecstasy. At the end of the rite, the volva would answer questions put to her by the celebrants. While in her trance she contacted the Gods for the purposes of divination. According to *Erik's Saga* her costume was made from different animal skins, including calf-skin boots and catskin gloves. She carried a staff with a knob on it, which was mounted with brass and had stones set around the base of the knob. As part of the rites, a ritual meal was prepared for her. Possibly there was a parallel between the calfskin boots and the dun bull hide worn by the Druid Mog-Ruith as part of a magic ceremony. The catskin gloves almost certainly connect with the Goddess Freya whose chariot, in Norse stories, was pulled by wildcats. Perhaps the catskin gloves also echo how in European legend the cat and the witch seem to go hand in hand—where there is a witch, there is also the cat familiar. Freya as the Deity Within the Wagon was also linked with the concept of the Three Mothers and concerned with fertility, the land, childbirth, and the raising of the family. We must also realize that seidr magic had its dark side; its practitioners were accused of magical dealings, cattle-blasting and other sorts of harm—all the things of which the old time witches were accused.

In the person of the Squirrel dancer, therefore, our tradition brings together all these strands of knowledge and creates from them a cohesive pattern or picture of the role or function of Squirrel within the Rites as a working member of the group. The person who dances Squirrel may be either male or female because we tend toward the old Germanic view, one noted by the Roman historian Tacitus in his *Histories*, that women were especially gifted with the powers of prophecy and divination.

Squirrel is a shaman but also more than a shaman; Squirrel at heart is the diviner, the seer who by his or her own efforts has found a unique path or way to both the Gods and the Underworld by the medium of chant and dance, building upon the keys provided by the group. The person who is Squirrel must awaken his or her own dormant powers, creating the aspect or shape that their guardian spirit or god will assume when meeting them in the trance state ecstasy of the rite. By doing this and, in effect, having been touched by the Godhead for a short while, they become an extension of that Godhead and, if they are a true medium-seer shaman dancer, the mouth of the Gods or the Goddess within the circle. Later on, they return to this world and once again become just another member of the group that has undertaken to worship the old Gods and the Goddess using the rites of the masked dancers.

Despite our references to old Nordic, Germanic, or Celtic mythology in order to provide a historical framework, the role of the Squirrel dancer is in reality a modern concept. There would have been no point in either claiming the mantle of or trying to re-create the cult of the Goddess Freya and the seer-priestesses that served Her. Pagan faiths were never centralized in the same way as the Christian Church. A person's faith was a highly individualistic one, a personal relationship between that being and their God. There were of course formal centers of worship in the form of temples, stone circles, and sacred groves, but this does not in any way distract from the basic premise that worship and faith were individual things along the lines of a pact or bargain between a person and the particular God or Goddess they had chosen to follow. Likewise, the role of Squirrel, and indeed all the other sacred animal or bird mask guises adopted by a group, must be developed as individual to that particular group and to no other. In effect, the founding members of the gathering are the ones who would have shaped the whole dance concept, creating it as they say it, while at the same time creating the pact between themselves and the old Gods and the Goddess to be built upon and later handed down to those who by an act of free will have chosen to follow them.

The Mask of Boar

Our Boar is no farmyard hog, which by any standards is ferocious enough, but the European wild boar, most certainly regarded alongside the stag as a ritually important animal. Throughout Celtic literature, there are references to the pig and the boar as a supernatural and magical animal, a hospitality symbol providing the champion's portion at the feast, a food of the Underworld that renewed itself every day. As a war symbol, right through from the Iron Age to the Romano-British period, the boar symbol was to be found decorating military equipment. Even though the boar/pig is recognized as an important Celtic hunting-food-battle-death ritualistic symbol, there was no overall Boar God figure. Boar was boar and sacred, and that was that, even though there are numerous examples of the boar as an anthropomorphic symbol,

even though there are known boar Gods such as Mercury Moccus of the Lingones district, or the boar Goddess Arduinna of the Ardennes.

Once again, it is a case of taking the little that is known and creating a role and a ritual pattern within the masked rites. In a supernatural/historical role, the boar of the Irish annals is also connected with shape-shifting and the ritual hunting of the invincible magical pig or boar. Also there were strong associations of the pig/boar with the leading of men to a sudden death and the Underworld. Also, there was the tradition of the Underworld pork that renewed itself each day, very much in the tradition of the boar Sechrimivar that renewed itself after being eaten by the heroes of the Norse Valhalla. Most certainly when Ottar the Simple, a worshiper of the Goddess

Freya, turned or disguised himself as Her boar, it could be that he donned a boar mask of a priest of the Vanir and as such, came under the protection of the Goddess.

When warriors used a boar crest or a boar mask as helmet and shield decoration, they were reminded of the ferocity and courage of the wild boar while at the same time filled with the same courage and ability to ignore wounds in the face of an enemy. The wearer of such decoration would be invoking the picture of the boar stalking the battlefield as the bringer of death to those who opposed or crossed swords with him. In fact, the symbolism of the boar was so well recognized in the ancient world that the Roman military adopted the boar crest as a legion unit standard. As part of the ritual of census taking, the Comitia Centuriata would be drawn up on the Campus Martius in military ranks for the Great State Sacrifice or *Suovetaurilia* of a pig, a sheep, and a bull as part of the ritual purification of the whole Roman male population.

Taking all preceding examples into account, there is certainly no question about the magical and mythological significance of the boar in early European history, and there can be no question that even though Britain was nominally a Christian country under the Celtic Church, successive Anglo-

Saxon and Jutish invasions would have re-introduced the boar mythos into the land. Thus the sacred boar of the Pagan Anglo-Saxons would have been passed down to their descendants, the English Witches.

Today we realize that there is a role for the boar-masked dancer within the circle, even though the boar may not be crucial to the actual rite. As the boar is associated with the Underworld, so is the dancer as one of the following who is led along the spiral path by Raven. Boar, by his association with death and the Underworld, is part of the mystic death and resurrection cycle, just as anyone connected with the rites as a whole must believe in the reincarnation of the human spirit as a way of progressing along the path of enlightenment and knowledge. The masked rites serve as a dramatic ritual that takes the dancers into a pseudo-death and then leads them back out again. From this, there will be a gradual build-up of knowledge and understanding of the relationship between the God, Man, and above all, life on this planet as we know it. This knowledge is not something gained from books or the writings of other people, but learned with the eyes of the seer/priest or priestess magician.

Of course, there is no way that we could recapture the instinctive understanding that they once had, nor if it

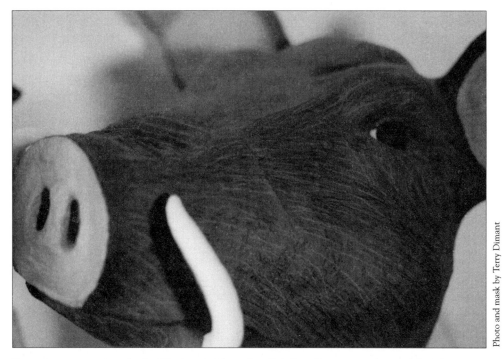

Photo and mask by Terry Dimant

Boar is associated with the Underworld, and will follow Raven on the spiral path.

was possible to do so would we even want to. They had something that gradually grew and expanded enough to bring in various cultures over a long time-span while still retaining the same old basic concept. We now have taken the old symbology and tried to get it to work for us once again. The difficulty is that we have to reshape our thinking to enable us to get under the skin, so to speak, of what is really nothing more than the magic of illusion—the magic where a person can don the mask of the boar and, in effect, become the prophetic boar/priest figure for the duration of the rite—not the easiest thing to do.

While Stag, Raven, and Squirrel have specific roles to play within the rites, Boar, like the others of the following, has no fixed status within the circle. He and the rest are the dancers. Still at times ordinary members of the following will take the lead or be called upon to dance the dance to the Goddess of Inspiration. Anything gained from it will be just as valid as anything gained from the more formal spiral, Raven, or Squirrel dance.

The group has a leader in Stag, an enchanter and soul-taker in Raven, as well as the prophet-shaman in Squirrel, but each dancer is a fully trained and fully initiated coven member in their right. Not everyone is suited to fill the role of Stag, Raven, or Squirrel; indeed, there are those who would hate to have to fill any of these roles, preferring to be one of the dancers. Each group will in time find its own Stag leader and its own Raven and Squirrel, but because they have taken these offices, that does not make them any better or more high-ranking than anyone else in the gathering. All it means is that they are more gifted and have a greater amount of the faculties that are inherent to us all, be they developed or not. All the dancers are people who have come together to work in a certain way, apart and at differient times from the rest of the coven gatherings. Having done this, they must remember that their first allegiance is to the coven proper and that the knowledge gained through these workings is the common property of all the coven members, initiates, or novices. What they are doing with the dance rites is for the coven and all the present and future members and, above all, to honor the Goddess in worship.

The Mask of Fox

With Fox we are again faced with reconstructing, because there is little information on the animal's ritual significance. "Fox" was used as a personal name by the Celts, as was born out by the classical writer Athenaeus Lavernian when he noted the Avernian chief Lovernus, son of Fox, in his works. A "Lovernus" is also mentioned on a set of pewter plates discovered in Appleford, Berkshire, England, and dated to the third century C.E. In Caernarvenshire, there was a stone inscribed "*Fili Ioverni Anatemore*," while in the Romano-British temple of Utley, Gloustershire, an altar was found with a fox reference. The old Strathclyde area of Lorne takes its name directly from Lovernous-son-of-Erc or "Fox-son-of-Erc," who colonized the area around 500 C.E., originally coming from Ireland where the Irish *loarn* or

fox had derived from the far older Lovernous.

Also, it is interesting to note that the body of the Lindlow Man wore a strip of fox fur as an arm band when he was ritually killed and his body placed in the peat bog.

The question of why the fox was held in high enough regard for people to use it as a personal name, as is shown by the few remaining altars and dedicatory tablets, might be answered in the image we have of fox as an animal. Its color is the first clue, taken with its sharp, pointed ears and narrow face which suggests craftiness—something to be watched while at the same time to be admired in a sneaky sort of way. The color of the fox might have led it to be associated with (in a sacrificial sense) the Sun God. Yet at the same time, because the fox is a sub-surface dweller, there is also a connection with the Underworld again. It may seem strange that a sly and somewhat malicious animal should be used to symbolize an aspect of divinity. The reason is quite simple: today we are brought up in the understanding that the Deity is an all-seeing, all-forgiving, omnipotent and benevolent God figure. In ancient and pre-Christian thought, this was far from the case. The Old Gods could be cruel, resentful of mankind, and more than ready to pull a man down for the sin of overweening pride and self-seeking glory. Worship was for the Gods and the Gods alone. Furthermore, the very air itself could be filled with invisible little imps and devils, or in the case of the Pagan population, evil and malign spirits that could be warded off or appeased with the appropriate rituals. Whereas in Christian theology you have an outright master of evil and sin in Satan or the Devil, in Pagan European thought the same spirit of evil was not defined in so clear-cut a way. Instead, it tended toward the Loki or Gwydion model: mischievous, yet at the same time having the power and the capability to help or harm mankind with the art of deceit and trickery. Most certainly, there are many examples to

Mask and photo by Karen St. Pierre

Fox was part of the old ways, a link with our Pagan past. This unusual rendition of fox utilizing feathers, fur, and metallic paint, is a modern link to the old Pagan ways.

be found in various mythologies of these demigods tricking the very Gods themselves out of certain gifts or arts and then passing them on to mankind in general or, in some cases, to a specific person.

It is little wonder that this crafty, sly, and vicious aspect or facet of the Gods was recognized, and that its earthly counterpart should be the fox, an animal given over to vicious killing fits for no apparent reason. In my case, I have known that a fox has been in an area for months, one afternoon going on a killing spree, biting the heads off half a dozen ducks and just leaving the bodies there, in much the same way the "Will of the Gods" would strike down some men and leave others of an equal status still standing.

Today, we no longer see the Goddess or the Gods with the same eyes as they were once seen in the past. Many things like livestock diseases, crop blights, and failures that were once put down to divine ill-will or punishment have been recognized, explained, and in many cases alleviated. Plagues, lead poisoning from water pipes, and so on—in fact, many of the things that were once called "divine punishment"—are now known to have been caused through our own ignorance and lack of understanding. Consequently, the fox-masked dancer of today bears little symbolic relationship to the fox-masked dancers of the past. Fox symbolized trickery and craft and in one sense has ceased to exist. Instead, Fox is the name for a masked dancer who is just one among the others who go to make up the full gathering.

Why not replace Fox with the mask of, say, Bulldog, Spaniel, or even Duck-billed Platypus, for that matter? Fox is included because Fox was part of the old form of rites, and today, in the re-creating of the sacred dance and sacred mask concept of worship, we feel that in a way, this is something of a memorial and link with our Pagan past. We recognize that time has tempered our perception of the Goddess and the Gods. We no longer lay at their feet the blame for results of acts of our own doing through ignorance or otherwise. At the same time, we know that the feeling of harmony, balance, understanding, and knowledge is an integral part of their worship and rites, and should be reflected back in our own make-up. In addition, bear in mind that there is in all of us a little of the fox, and we should not only have the ability to contain it but to use it as well.

The Mask of Goose

Over the centuries, the mythos of the sacred goose has become jumbled with other concepts, gradually losing the element that made it sacred once. To try and regain all that was lost and at the same time take away what does not belong to it is a nigh-impossible task, certainly beyond the scope of this present work. Yet it is still possible to create something of what it once stood for from the few pieces of the sacred goose mythos that are left. I once looked at a modern Breton-made statuette owned by an acquaintance. Aside from its attractive artistic qualities, the first thing that struck me was that I was able to "read" it because, in effect, it was nothing more than a series of Pagan symbols brought together. Whether the artist who created the statuette knew what he or she was saying, I don't know—all the right symbols were there and many were just where you would expect them to be. It was a statuette of the enthroned Goddess Herself. On the back of the throne was emblazoned the noontime sun, which of course you would expect to find, but, unexpectedly, it was the actual sun itself and not a solar wheel disc or sun symbol. More interesting, among all the other symbols were two geese, one decorating each side of the throne and each with an extended neck and head looking upward to the Goddess. From what is known of the role of the goose in Celtic mythology, one would expect to find the goose at the feet of the Goddess and gazing up at Her with a look of adoration and worship because, like the raven, the wild goose bore away the souls of the winter dead.

In this symbolism, the wild goose becomes an aspect of the Mother as

Pale-Faced Goddess of the cold North, the one "whose breath is borne upon the chill winds of the North." Here an observation of the natural world becomes an allegory within the mythology of the Old Faith. You only have to stand on any esturial saltings watching the first flights of the incoming wild geese honking away as they land to realize that even today there is still a certain amount of magic in their arrival—even though we know their migratory habits and the vast distances they fly to winter here in Britain. The geese's coming heralded the coming of winter when the shadow of death would stalk across the land claiming the old, the very young, the sick, and the weak. When the wild geese flew off, it would herald the coming of spring. As the land's ancient inhabitants watched the vee formations flying off into the early morning sun and not returning until late next autumn, they said that the geese took with them the souls of the winter's dead as they returned to the halls and the throne of the Pale-Faced Goddess. With the first cold blasts of winter felt in the winds, came the goose and death, and with their going, came the first hints of gentle, kindly reign of the Summer King (providing of course that the Gods were not angry and sent storms, gales, and general bad weather).

In North America, natives observed that the going of the geese brought winter and the returning birds brought with them the spirit of the coming summer. Either way, they remain a living, breathing symbol of the faith.

Perhaps the most famous sacred geese in the Classical world were the Capitoline Hill geese of Rome, who were, of course, domesticated birds. They were credited with the saving of the Capitoline garrison by alerting them one night during a siege by an army of Gauls, who had taken the rest of Rome except for this one strongpoint. (I suppose it is only fair to say that this is perhaps the only really concrete, documented example of the ancient sacredness of the goose.)

Again, we take the few known facts and create a supposition based on the knowledge that we do have, creating a role for Goose within the rites in the same way as for Stag, Raven, and Squirrel. To include Goose means that we are harking back to old imagery of one facet of the Goddess. Goose may symbolize the overall concept of death, the soul, and eventual rebirth of that soul, with Goose as the bearer-away-of-souls of the newly dead. With their return, they bring something of the soul that they once carried off to the place of rest before rebirth.

Some purists might say that none of this is in the strict Craft tradition; in this they are right, but I challenge them to define just what are the "strict traditions" of the Craft. Though the magical goose belongs more to the Celtic Otherworld concept than the Craft, the Craft is dynamic enough to accept individual coven or clan-created rites and concepts, yet still maintain within its framework the overall concept of what being a Witch means. With this in mind, when the time comes for me to cash in my number, I only hope that somewhere among all those geese visiting our winter shore will be the one magical goose sent by the Goddess to take my soul home.

The Mask of Owl

Owl's ritual personality draws more upon the Greco-Roman world than the Germanic or Celtic; its historical precedent is Athena's owl. Yet a sacred owl fits well into the ranks of the masked following. First, Owl has the symbolic attribute of wisdom. Additionally, in both Great Britain and Europe there is a strong body of belief that the owl was a bird of omen, usually connected with or announcing a death. Certainly in the past the owl and the Witch have been associated with each other, even though the owl was nearly always pictured or placed in the background. Since the owl is not a traditional Witch's "familiar," there must have been some other explanation for the Witch/Owl association. Here we approach the true concept of the owl as a magical bird and see the way that the Owl-masked dancer can

fill a particular role within the masked assembly.

Both the Witch and the Owl are creatures of the night. Most owls hunt at night, taking rats, mice, voles, and other small creatures. To hear a rat squeal at night, breaking the silence, can be quite a scary thing. The eerie hooting of an owl, followed by the squealing scream of some small animal in fear of its very life, would suggest something more than that to a superstition-filled mind. The people who heard it, because of the nature of their upbringing and thinking concerning the supernatural, would tend to regard this as proof positive that the ill-omened owl was carrying off another dammed soul to its mistress, the Goddess who presided over the Underworld.

Meanwhile, Church-inspired propaganda filled the night with witches holding their satanic rites and vowing to help their master, the Devil, to entice unwary but good Christian souls from the true path of belief and ultimate salvation. Even though the stereotyped medieval witch worshiped the Devil and had made a pact with him that in exchange for some gift, power, or what-have- you, at the end of a fixed period of time, the Devil would claim the witch's soul. When folk huddled together at night and heard the hooting of the owl and the scream of torment after, it might suggest to a conditioned and susceptible mind that another unwilling witch's soul was being carried off by their master, the Devil. They would cross themselves and murmur, "Thank God we're all pious Christians and under the protection of Holy Mother Church."

As hard as it is for us to slip under the skin and into the minds of medieval people's way of thinking and conditioning as preached by Holy Mother Church, we have to try if we are to have any inkling of how natural phenomena could come to be seen as "witchcraft" and satanic evil.

On one level, the owl was once regarded as a sacred bird dedicated to the Goddess, or one of the physical guises donned or adopted by the Goddess to secretly visit or watch over Her following during their act of worship. On another level, this same owl and its

Chas S. Clifton, mask made by Martin Anthony

The owl is a bird of omen.

hooting was a physical omen that death was about to claim the soul of another one of Her worshipers, either as a known or an unknown but suspected follower. In this light, the old spirit of the owl with its Goddess association and its Goddess-inspired fund of knowledge and wisdom fits in very well with the overall concept of what the masked rites are all about.

Translated into modern terms, the masked owl dancer might be perhaps the oldest serving member of the gathering, providing the "wise old owl" figure of the meeting. Even though Owl would not have the same openly displayed status as Stag, Raven, and Squirrel, she or he is the one looked to for advice when things seem not to be working as expected. Owl passes on knowledge gained from the workings to the newcomers of the group. In short, this person would be the one to carry in his or her head the whole of the concept, the whole of the techniques used in the workings of the rites, and above all, be ready to volunteer this information when it is called for and not before. Owl is the semi-hidden guardian of the rites, as well as being the custodian of the concept and the purity of the rites.

With this change we are in fact following the far older tradition of the Craft by adapting the mechanics of the concept to suit the times in which we are at present living. When there is need for another change, the Eternal Goddess through Her sacred bird will sow the first seeds of that knowledge and understanding, then leave it to future coven followings to nurse it to fruition.

The Mask of Cat

The cat, paradoxically, has been at times accorded near-divine status, as well as being regarded as a valued household pet and friend. In later ages, it was simultaneously associated with the Devil and all his works, yet it was something useful to have around. Poor old cat was judged guilty by association. The association between cats and humans has been a long one, yet no one has gotten really close to the mind of the cat or even understood the cat in the same way as we have come to understand the dog.

In ancient Egypt the cat was closely identified with the Goddess Bastis, who was Herself portrayed as a cat-headed goddess of fertility, pleasure, and maternity. There is also a strong body of evidence that the cat was also associated with both Isis and Osiris. Indeed, the Roman historian Plutarch recorded that to the Egyptians, the tomcat represented the sun, and the queen, the moon, and there still is in existence a tomb painting of the God Ra represented as a cat eating up the snake of darkness. Some of the sistra used in the temples very often had female cat figures on them; during eclipses, these would be shaken to aid and encourage the Goddess Bastis to eat up the darkness and restore the light. On a more prosaic level, in the land of stored grain and granaries, the ability of the cat as a vermin killer took on a great significance and the affection that these useful pets were held in is attested by the sheer volume of mummified cat remains that have been found.

The Greeks, on the other hand, understood the value of the cat for its rodent-killing abilities, but never set much store by cats in a religious or mystic sense, regarding the creature as something useful to have around. However, the Romans regarded the cat as a symbol of freedom: the old Roman fortress of Car Vicense in the Netherlands still commemorates this in the name of Kattewyk or Cat Town.

In the case of the Celts, one only has to look up the law passed by the Welsh king Hywel Da circa 936 C.E. to gain some insight and understanding of their importance. This fixed the penalty for killing a cat firmly within the framework of the law, as well as requiring payment of a compensatory value which, considering the ability of the cat as a rodent killer, was poetically assessed in a measure of grain. So after enjoying centuries of worship as a semi-divine animal and valued for its ability as a controller of rodent pests, how did poor old puss become a cruelly treated and vilified "satanic" creature?

One reason may be the connection of the Norse fertility goddess Freya with cats. Her mythical chariot was pulled by European wildcats, larger and fiercer than domestic cats, but similar looking. At one time, of course, her worship was a competitor to the Catholic Church, which was not as universal as it would have liked to think. This was the same church whose leader, Pope Innocent VIII, first legalized the persecution of witches and with it, the persecution of the cat. One

of the main threads running through the history of the whole period of the witch persecutions is that the cat as a familiar was the main instrument in bringing about all sorts of misfortunes in the name of the Devil. Sudden deaths, miscarriages, madness, crop failures, outbreaks of disease both human and animal—you name it, and the witch with her or his cat was to blame for it.

The Church itself inspired and backed anti-witch hysteria which in turn, during medieval times, led to the writing of such books as *Beware The Cat,* which issued the solemn warning that a witch could take on the shape of nine different cats one after the other. It wasn't any use killing one cat—all nine had to be killed. So widespread and firmly held was this conviction that it led to many cases of cats being brought to trial under the witchcraft acts just in case poor old puss was a shape-changing witch. Indeed, such was the dread of cats in France that on St. John's Day it was customary to ritually burn sacks-full of cats in his honor. Even today, on May 14, the Ypres Cat Festival is held in that Belgian city, and toy cats are thrown from the town belfry with little ribbons tied round their necks which later are exchanged for prizes. This is merely a humane commemoration of the ten-centuries-old custom of throwing live cats from a tower to prove that the citizens of Ypres were "good Christians." In the same vein, both in France and Germany, cats were often garlanded and afterwards offered up as a ritual sacrifice/thanks offering at harvest time.

On an individual level, some poor, lonely old woman, possibly half-crippled with arthritis, would keep a pet cat for company, and it was probably the only living thing in years that offered her any sort of affection. When her neighbors—out of sheer spite, fear, or perhaps greed for her cottage or little bit of land—wanted to get rid of her, they simply charged her with being a witch. The evidence? "The old hag kept a cat, and we all know who the cat serves, don't we?" and for this crime, a probable burning for both of them. Perhaps in a way, the cat had his revenge; without the large numbers of cats needed to keep the rat population down, the bubonic plague of the fifteenth century spread that much faster.

Although the cat is no longer regarded as a manifestation of Satan. there is still a residual belief in the supernatural abilities and aspects of the cat—but this cat lore is totally inconsistent. For some, a black cat is considered lucky, yet to old-time seamen the black cat was seen as a bringer of bad weather, shipwreck, fire, disaster, and probably all sorts of other complaints ranging from flat feet to toothache. If the ship's cat ran away, it was a sure sign that the ship was making her last voyage. In the Far East, great faith was always placed in sending a tortoiseshell cat to the top of the mast to chase away the storm demons. There is much folklore concerning the cat's influence on the weather along the lines of "If the cat turns its tail toward the fire, this is a sure sign of a coming frost." Licking its tail meant that rain was on the way. Old wives' tales they may seem to be; on the other hand, cats are hypersensitive to changes in the weather pattern and do respond with changed behavior.

Considering how the cat has suffered at the hands of bigoted mankind because once other humans placed it on a pedestal of semi-divinity, there can be no question that the cat firmly belongs within the ranks of the ritual animals. In the past a Goddess was portrayed with cats harnessed to Her cart, another Goddess was represented as a cat-headed deity, and today we should remember that cats are a creature of the night and sacred to the Goddess of the night. Therefore, accursed are they who harm the cat, for by doing so, they harm the Goddess. Remembering their history, we should honor them by wearing the mask of Cat within the sacred circle. Like us, they in their own way know something of and render their own form of worship to the Goddess.

The Mask of Ram

In many ways the mythos of the ram has become mixed up and intertwined with the mythos of the roebuck in the thicket. An additional mixing in of the goat-foot Pan figure has made the two figures somewhat interchangeable in the mythological sense.

So what is the role of Ram within the rites? By turning the clock back and looking into the past and, in particular, at the roots of the sacrificed Divine King mythos and the way it has spilled over into the old Anglo-Saxon witchcraft concept, our understanding of the ram becomes more sharply defined. Ram is nothing more or less than another substitute for the Divine King sacrifice which segued into the Witch concept of the old substitute blood price paid by the magister of the coven every seven years.

In the earliest concept of the ram, we see the strong and virile male ani-

mal fighting to preserve his dominance over the females of the flock in much the same way as King Stag fights to preserve and maintain his rights over the does of the herd. Instead of being set in the wild, it is set against the background of the semi-domesticated flocks of sheep owned by the community. Translated into fertility-cum-religious terms, you have King Ram from whose strength and virility the flocks increase. The older he gets, the more he is challenged, until he is no longer strong enough to beat off the attacks of the younger rams—in short, the Young Horned King superseding the old Horned King of the May Eve sacrifice. Even though there has been a change from the old to the new, or perhaps because of the change, the flock, or in human terms, the clan, is stronger by increasing in numbers. Once again, it all boils down to the old concept of the strength of any group being gauged by the strength of its leader. As long as he was strong, so was the group. When he weakened, so did the group. It was from this line of reasoning that the concept of sacrificing the leader, chief, or king while still in his prime arose, for to let him grow old while still holding office would in a sympathetic magical way weaken the tribe or clan.

Of course, the Goddess and the old Gods still had to have their dues in the form of a blood sacrifice, a life in exchange for the blessing of life and prosperity for the clan. What better way to pay than with the ram, symbolic of the Horned God and living a life that was in accord with the magico-religious thinking of the ancient society? The ram served a twofold purpose: on the one hand, a recognizable life form that symbolized an outward and visible manifestation of the God. As such, the ram could be dedicated to the Gods as a substitute for the still-strong leader. Killed, and with the God's portion burned in the flames of the sacred fire, the remains of the carcass would be cooked, providing the food for the feast where part of the body of the old Living God on Earth was ritually consumed. The priesthood and the elders of the clan partook of the courage and wisdom of the king, now magically transferred to the body of the ram and eaten by them along

with the meat. The tribe or clan still had a leader who was strong and virile, with the added advantage of being a year older and a year wiser, so in effect the religious obligations of the group were fulfilled without actually having to sacrifice a life.

In the same train of thought, the skull of the dead ram became a symbol of the Gods, since it could be fixed to a pole, making it a totem symbol of the clan. Because it was a symbol of the Gods, very often the skull would be buried in the entrance of the circle as the ritual guardian and gateway sacrifice of the sacred site where the priesthood of the group gathered to offer worship and come face to face with the Goddess and the Gods while in shamanistic spirit form.

From these practices arose the old Craft tradition of "something for something." Whatever a person takes from the Craft, a price has to be paid for it. In other words, you take something and give something in return. This includes the simple leaving of a small coin in token payment for the cutting out of an ash stang, to the more formal concept of the blood substitute every seven years during the leadership of a coven magister. Once the rank of coven magister was in effect the same as the Divine Sacrificial King. When the kingship and priesthood evolved into two separate functions, the role of the priesthood changed. The leader became the sacrificial incarnate God-figure of the gathering and in effect, the old divine substitute, even though by then the concept of the Divine King Sacrifice had fallen into disuse.

What used to happen was that the Magister of the coven was supposed to offer himself up as a sacrifice every seven years in the light of the Seven-Year King concept. Then the concept of the ram as the recognizable and acceptable sacrifice came into being. Every seventh year the coven leader named the ram after himself, thereby placing everything on the ram's head. As the priest of the rites, it was his duty to sacrifice the ram as the blood payment demanded of him for his priesthood.

Today, by recalling the ram and its place within the rites, we turn away from the sacrificial aspect of the beast and instead look toward the symbolic meaning of the ram. No longer does the magister have to offer blood as the payment at the end of the seventh year; instead, repeating the oath of office has been recognized as sufficient. Rather than regard the ram as a sacrificial beast, we should look to the mask of ram as one of the masks of the Godhead that symbolizes to mankind a physical form of an abstract concept that gradually became known to us as the mythos of the Gods. For this reason, Ram has his place within the ranks of the masked following of the Goddess. Ram is now one of the masks through which the Gods can speak, and the wearer of the mask sometimes is the vehicle through trance by which the age-old Goddess-inspired wisdom is handed down to us as part of our birthright.

The Mask of Hare

Three magical traditions come together in the mask of Hare. First, we have the mystical animal sacred to the Moon Goddess. Second, we have the "mad" March hare, a reference to insanity in a magical or prophetic form. Third is the concept of shapeshifting, with a special reference to the Druids and to one of the shapes that the old-time witches were reputed to assume on coming or going from their coven meetings. All of these combine to make up one distinctive aspect or face of the sacred hare.

The hare as such was always considered sacred to the Goddess in Her aspect of Diana, Goddess of the hunt. (The eating of the hare was always taboo to the Celtic races.) Among the old-time witch gatherings, the eating of the hare was and is, so far as I know, still taboo today. None of the people I have met or

worked with would dream of hunting and killing a hare, let alone eat one.

Even today, in certain cultures there is a tradition that a mad person has been touched by the finger of God and as such it is the duty of every person to make sure they come to no harm. One-time European thinking held that the moon could turn people crazy, hence the expression "lunatic" for one driven mad by the moon or the Lunar goddess. There is more than a grain of truth in this if you regard this form of madness as the frenzied Goddess-inspired prophetic seizures that have been known to take hold of people during meetings. Very often most of what a person in this stage of religious ecstasy says makes very little sense at all, yet occasionally they come out with something that is pure inspiration, or they start prophesying some future event in great detail and then suddenly slip back into gibberish again. What they have foretold occurs with an uncanny accuracy. The claim to be as "mad as a March hare" is based on nothing more than the extravagance of the hares' courting and mating habits, which seen by the light of the full moon, seem to be a half-battle, half-dance ritual performed in part to the Moon Goddess.

The other peculiarity about the hare is the fact that it has no home in the sense of a burrow or den. Even when giving birth to its young, the only shelter the hare needs is long grass or other foliage. Unlike the rabbit in its warren, there is no way you can net-trap the hare using ferrets. The hare starts in any piece of open ground and the next moment it is gone, seemingly coming from nowhere and then disappearing again. Little wonder that in time the hare would come to symbolize the spirit of the shaman/magician changing into an animal, disappearing when seen, and then changing back into human form again. After all, a person able to do this would not need a home while in animal form, would they?

Lore and superstition grew up around the hare and its association with the Goddess and the Otherworld spirits. Unfortunately, like so many of these things, most of the lore of the hare has

been lost to us. All that remains are the few vague hints and references garnered from writings on the old traditions. What we now have to do is to re-awaken the old spirit of Hare and from a reappraisal of the remaining body of evidence, create a modern role within a body of modern rites.

So what would we expect from the role of Hare today? Very little in the sense of Hare having a great esoteric role or meaning within the hierarchy of the dancers. By any normal reckoning, Hare should be just another dancer of the Following. The role fits someone who is often a "sensitive." By the word "sensitive" I mean a person who is gifted with the faculty and ability of seeming to grab information from out of the very air itself in a way that is positively uncanny to behold. It is this sort of person who comes closest to symbolizing what the concept of Hare should be when translated into human terms.

No amount of training or study can create this faculty in a person; either they have it or they don't. The rest of us must expect that on occasions the person who is donning the mask of Hare will suddenly take over the rite. As unpredictable as this may seem because it is Hare that is doing the leading, it is still within the pattern of the rites. In Chapter Six, "The Dances of the Following," I will return to this theme; for now, it is enough to say that the rest of the dancers must follow the lead of Hare because the Hare dancer will be following their traditional role.

If the group is recognizing Hare in their true role, then Hare has always been the solitary one who has dedicated itself to the Goddess in a more personal way than the others of the group. Hare is the servant of the Goddess on earth, it is to Her and to Her alone that Hare opens itself up, it is Her inspiration that leads Hare into a rite that is outside the normal workings. Where there is a true Hare, then there is an instrument of the Goddess that she can work through to lead the gathering into that mystic union of both mind and spirit between the Goddess and Her congregation. Those of us not gifted with a "sensitive" within our ranks to fill the role of a true Hare must accept the next best thing and honor our Hare dancer, while at the same time realizing that there are limitations placed on the role. Hare in this case becomes a symbol of the reality as it could have been, given the right circumstances. So the reality in most groups is that the Hare dancer is one of the thirteen dancers and the outward symbol of what was once a special tradition within the special masked rites. Hare being Hare and totally unpredictable, one day the Goddess will inspire Hare to fulfill their proper or traditional role, and take Hare by the hand and lead them, and through Hare, the rest of the congregation, into an act of worship of Her choosing.

The Mask of Mare

The mask of Mare symbolizes one of the main myths within the traditional Witch faith, but this is only one aspect of the ancient and widespread deification and veneration of the horse among our ancestors. In the past, many cults were formed around the horse as a religious symbol, but as far as we are concerned, only one aspect is relevant to us in a religious sense. The mythos likely itself came from the Celts. Just how and when it became assimilated into Anglo-Saxon or English Witchcraft, no one knows, but assimilated it was, and it took on a form that is peculiar to Witchcraft alone. It parallels the way that the Witch Faith adopted the concept of the Castle that spins without motion between two worlds and made both an article of faith within the framework and traditions of the Witch religion.

In the first instance, the horse we are looking at is the fabled "Night-Mare," the steed ridden by the Horned God on the night of the Wild Hunt, driving souls into the Underworld. In Christian terms, it is the spectral animal used by the Devil when he rides out—also in some ways, a linear descendant of the steeds used by the four dread horsemen of the Apocalypse—much in the same vein as the mount of the headless horseman reputed to haunt various parts of the country. In short, this horse is an ill-omened, spectral beast long connected with death, evil, hauntings, and the Underworld. Indeed, such is the connection of this horse with fear, dread, and things that go bump in the night, that a bad dream that wakes up the sleeper in a cold sweat and scared to death is still called a nightmare.

So just what is this creature that over the centuries has filled the minds of so many with dread? Again, it is part of an old faith or tradition that has been modified by Christianity until, in the end, it projects the image the early Church wished to portray while at the same time still maintaining its age-old concept and meaning—the same concept to which we still adhere today.

Some Witches envision the nightmare as a coal-black steed, wild-eyed, with foam-flecked mouth and with hoofs lashing out in a frenzied manner. On her back is the dark rider, horned, grim-faced, merciless, without one ounce of pity in Him. Snapping round her heels are the very Underworld hounds themselves, white of coat, red in ear, and sharp in fang, impatiently waiting for the sounding of the horn by the hunter to start them off on their arrow-straight path to their chosen target. They symbolize an act of revenge by the Horned God against the evildoer cursed by the priesthood for the harm or hurt they have done to the tribe, clan, or on a lesser level, the coven. In the same way as the Church personified evil in the form of the Devil and at the same time gave over the souls of wrongdoers to Him as a punishment, so do we, but instead of separating good and evil into two aspects, we recognize the one aspect able to judge and give vengeance where vengeance is due. Once the priesthood of the clan, or at a much later date the Witches, came to symbolize the Hounds of Hell, and the Maid or Priestess of the coven

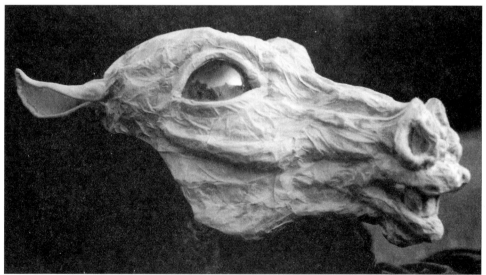

Mask and photo by Robin Larsen,

A plaster mare mask under construction. Looking at this mask, it is easy to visualize the dark rider's steed on the Wild Hunt.

symbolized the night-mare. Through her, the group works a ritual that lays before the Horned God the reason for wanting vengeance; the formal laying-on of the curse is itself part of an act of revenge. Finally the curse is sent home in the name of the dark side of the Horned God by the priestess in the coven's name.

The Wild Hunt is more formal, but related. Its spiritual aim is to rid the countryside of the ghosts of the dead and lead them through the gates of the Underworld—in the sense of modern Candlemas rites, to bury the last of the old year in preparation for the coming year. This harks back to the old belief that the spirits of the dead were all around, able to interfere directly in the lives of the people, hence the concept of ancestor worship. It would have been the priesthood's duty to drive these spirits into the Underworld. Again we see the Horned God in His aspect as the Prince of the Mound and the tomb/entrance gateway to the Underworld, mounted on his coal-black steed, and then riding forth to aid mankind by conducting the souls of the dead to where they rightfully belonged.

Today's physical manifestation of this concept is embodied in the Witch tradition of the Wild Hunt. In the past, knowing well the workings of Chris-tianized but still superstition-filled minds, often the Wild Hunt would be used to scare the hell out of the local population, keeping them well away from the coven members making their way home after the Candlemas meeting. Today, though the imagery of the Horned Hunter and His Night-Mare is no longer invoked in the same way, the old concept is still recognized in the Candlemas rites when the shade of the old year, symbolized by the old fire, is put out and a new flame lit. One year is dead and gone forever, never to return, while another is about to begin. Thus the cycle of life runs the full circle from birth to maturity and then death, only to be born again.

Considering the way that the image of the Mare has embedded itself into the fabric of the faith, there is no way that the Mare could be left outside the sacred masked gathering. To do so would have taken away from the faith something that has been handed down from generation to generation, while at the same time removing a symbol of a still-valid concept. By having the mask of Mare within the ranks of the dancers, we are paying tribute to an old phase of what was once the accepted rites while establishing the fact that there is more to the rites than just a mask.

The Mask of Hound

The mask of Hound continues the Night-Mare mythos. Once again we encounter the concept of judgment and action against individuals or groups, both in this world and the next. All this is done in the name of the Gods, by the servants of the Gods. We must realize that the old priesthood saw themselves in a different light than we do today. To them, anyone who endangered the existence of the group in any way was a sworn enemy of that group. Endangering the group might occur not only in a physical way, but also by acts of blasphemy, desecration of tombs and sacred sites, and—most importantly—the breaking of tribal or group taboos. To us today, this may seem a strange state of mind to understand and come to grips with, but we must try to reach some sort of rapport with this thinking if we are to understand how the concept evolved. To the Celts, the conviction of an afterlife was so strong that debts run up in this life were often pledged to be repaid in the next as a normal course of events. In much the same way, the ancient Egyptians would often damage the tomb paintings of a hated landowner or lord who had had idealistic afterlife scenes painted on the walls of his tomb in the conviction that this would be the life he would lead in the next world. By cutting, say, the thumb (in the painting) of the owner of the tomb, in a magical way the soul of that person would be crippled in the same manner. Likewise, the old priesthood would regard cursing an enemy as something that could be carried on beyond the grave, with the soul still affected by the curse placed on it, thus blighting their afterlife.

The old priesthood saw itself as the custodians of the spirit of the community. They would be the healers of the sick, the smellers-out of wrongdoers, the guardians and enforcers of tribal taboos—the human equivalent of the Hounds of Hell. In the name of the Gods, they would hound a person both body and soul for something that was against the Gods and the community. While on one hand there was a formalized tribal-cum-state religion administered by a hierarchy of priestly counselors under the leadership of the king, or at an earlier day a priest/king, on the other hand then was the old wise man or woman at a village or settlement level. It would be to them that the community would turn, unorganized in a formal sense and far apart from the state dignitaries who probably would not have recognized their claim to any sort of priesthood in the first place. Steeped in the lore of the countryside and definitely wise in a community sense, these would have been the people who held the keys to the spiritual life and well-being of the community, formed by a tight-knit collection of individuals. Most likely these wise ones would have hung on to the old knowledge long after Christianity superseded the old Pagan faith among the ruling classes, the faith that later would be branded as "Devil worship," and its followers, the "evil witches."

From the preceding it can be seen that the mask of Hound would only be invoked in specific circumstances, along with the Night-Mare and the Horned God/Rider figure, as part of the act of cursing. We stress that if this type of ritual is ever used, it must be as a last resort. Today, though the mechanics of the act of a formal and ritual cursing are known, the mask of Hound is no longer involved only with this sort of working. At Candlemas (February 2) the emphasis has changed, but the old concept of a time for cleansing is still observed, now centered on the laying of the spirit of the old year rather than the ghosts of our ancestors.

Nevertheless, we still keep the tradition of the old Wild Hunt, though in a more subdued form. For the mad rush away from the working site, there should be the feeling that the members are indeed the hounds being unleashed for this madcap time of running until out of breath. Very often things happen at this time that are the opposite of what was intended, and what started off as nothing more than a token performance is picked up by the scruff of the neck by the Goddess and turned into reality. The members are taken over by events and become the living descendants of the old-time Hounds of Hell, running once again the old, old hunt.

The mask of Hound reminds us that the ability, the knowledge, and the understanding on how to place a curse on an enemy of the group is still there. If something goes wrong at some time, and something from the other side leaks through and causes all sorts of psychic nastiness and trouble, the group should have the experience and knowledge to bind whatever it is that has come through and chase it back from whence it came. Part of this type of ritual working would involve all the group mentally donning the mask of Hound and once again representing the four-legged servants of the Horned Hunter, Prince of the Mound and Underworld, binding something that is not of this world to its own place.

The Mask of Swan

Often it seems that the mask of Swan sounds a discordant note among the other masks. In many ways this is deliberate because though the swan is not a magical bird in the Witch sense, it has a distinct air of magic about it. Two elements come together in the magical Swan mythos. It recalls the so-called twilight of the old Gods of Ireland and the coming of the new Christian faith.

As the monkish fabulists would have it, a Christian saint broke the spell cast over the swan children of Lêr by their stepmother Aeife, thus freeing them from a Pagan spell. As is usual with any sort of ancient myth, the old Gods of the tale are seen to be in human form rather than an ill-defined formless omnipotent power, and so it is with this story concerning the sea god Lêr, dweller in the mound of Fion-

machaidl or the hill of the White Field. Following the death of his beloved wife, Bobd the Red, king of all the gods of Ireland, sent Lêr a message offering him one of his foster daughters in marriage. Lêr chose the eldest foster daughter, Aebh, for his bride. Four children were born of this marriage: the first, a daughter named Finola; the second, a son named Aed.

At the final birthing, which unfortunately killed Aebh, were born her twin sons, Fiachra and Conn. Once again, in the name of friendship, Bobd the Red offered one of his foster daughters to Lêr as a wife. This time Lêr chose the second eldest daughter, Aeife, as his bride. The marriage, happy at first, soon soured when Aeife proved to be barren, while the children of her foster sister grew up to become favorites of both Lêr and the people of the Goddess Danu. Aeife, like the perennial stepmother of fairy tale fame, saw in the children a threat to her relationship with her husband. At first, she hoped that death would soon claim the children. Then she actively plotted to have them murdered by her servants, who much to their credit refused. Aeife was left with only one course, to use magic against them.

Taking the children to bathe in the waters of Lough Derravargh, County Meath, she uttered a spell over them and touched each one with her Druidic wand, changing them into swans. The one thing her magical powers were unable to do was to rob the children of their powers of speech and thought.

Aeife, though threatened with the anger of their father and Bobd the Red, still refused to undo her magic, but she did tell them how long they would be held in this condition. For three hundred years they would dwell in the form of swans on Lough Derravach; another three hundred years they would spend on the sea of Moyle; and then three hundred years on the Irros Doonann. The only consolation that they would have was that they would still keep their human minds and voices, and that they would sing the sweetest songs the world had ever heard.

Aeife, speeding back to Lêr, told him that the children had drowned, but Lêr did not believe her and so jour-

neyed to the lake where he heard four swans talking among themselves in human voices. They, recognizing their father, told him what had happened to them and pleaded with him to use his own magic to lift the spell that had been put upon them.

Neither Lêr nor Bobd the Red—even though he was king of the Gods—could undo the magic binding them. All they could do was punish Aeife for her treachery by making her swear under oath to name the thing she most dreaded to be. Having sworn under oath, she was obliged to answer and with one blow from the wand of Bobd the Red, Aeife became what she most feared to be and fled from the court a shrieking demon of the air.

To cut a long story short, the years of the children's tribulations dragged on and on, and it was during this time that Saint Patrick came to Ireland and banished the old Gods forever. When the children of Lêr were free to return to their old home, they found it empty and deserted. Searching long and in vain for their relatives and kin, they in the end gave up hope of ever seeing them again and sadly returned to the Isles of Glory where eventually they were found by Saint Coemhoc.

After listening to their story, he took them back to his church, telling them of the new faith that he represented. Converted to Christianity, they consented to be baptized, and on being sprinkled with the holy water, Aeife's spell was finally broken and the four children reassumed their human form. Because of their great age, they soon all died and were buried in the same grave.[2]

We suggested earlier that the mask of Swan seems to have very little in common with the other sacred masks. Looked at again, the myth of the swan contains within it all the elements that go to make up the concept of the masked rituals. We see the Swan/Priestess with her Druidic wand, the magic spell that was placed on the children, turning them into bird form while at the same time leaving them with the powers of human speech and thought; the age-old concept that once a person's fate had been invoked and placed on them, the powers of the old Gods or even the Goddess could do very little to remove it; and, finally, a reminder that the punishment placed upon Aeife teaches that magic used for its own ends will eventually demand a price from the user and that what is invoked can boomerang back on the practitioner in an unexpected way.

When the mask of Swan is worn, it suggests that practice of magical workings involves both the practitioner and the target of the workings in what is being done, and that a person had better be sure that what they are doing is right because the abuse of power can and will in the end lead to retribution. For these reasons the mask of Swan has its place within the masked rites of worship and the gaining of knowledge and understanding that is the primary aim of being a follower of the Goddess.

Notes

1. The illustrations heading each section in this chapter are an example of badges that could be made and worn when masks are not available. See page 127 for further discussion on the use of badges as an alternative to masks.

2. For a fuller version of the story of Aeife and the swan children, one cannot do better than to read *Celtic Myth and Legend* by Charles Squire.

Raven Mask and Concept by Robin Larsen,
Wings and Costume by Aletta Vett and Vanya Franck

Leather Raven Mask by Jorge Añón,
Courtesy of Sears Eldredge

Raven Mask: Papier Mâché over
FabricForm™ by Robin Larsen

Leather Cat Mask by Jorge Añón,
Courtesy of Sears Eldredge

Stag Mask by Robin Larsen,
Headdress by Chris LaBarca

Fabric and Silk Cat Mask by Robin Larsen

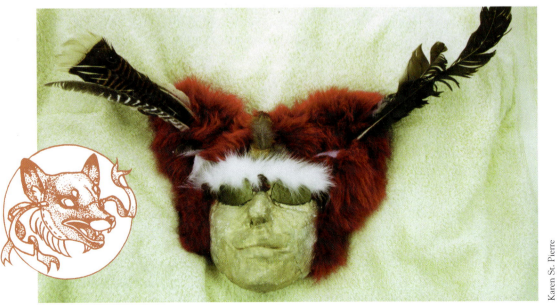

Fox Spirit Mask with fur, feathers, and metallic gold face by Karen St. Pierre

Leather Ram Mask by Jorge Añón, Courtesy of Sears Eldredge

Wendy Crowe

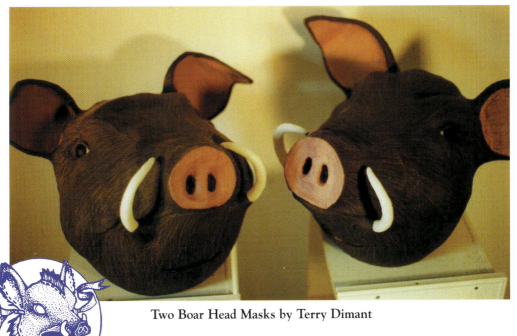

Two Boar Head Masks by Terry Dimant

Terry Dimant

Leather Owl Mask by Jorge Añón,
Courtesy of Sears Eldredge

Leather Hound Mask by Jorge Añón,
Courtesy of Sears Eldredge

Papier Mâché Nightmare Mask by Robin Larsen

Chapter Four

Reaching the Unconscious

The "common unconscious" is a faculty shared by every living person. Many may regard this as a somewhat improbable statement, but nevertheless it is a true one. Every person has built into their nervous system the ability to reach the basic shamanic ("first-state") trance; furthermore, this trance follows a common pattern irrespective of the race, color, or nationality of the trance subject.

In the first stage of the trance, a person often experiences a vision of circular bands of light seen against a dark background. In the second stage, there is a distinct vision of a series of circular zig-zags. In the third stage, superimposed in the center of the zig-zag pattern, there is a grid formation. At the fourth stage, there is a combination of all three effects, coupled with images of things that are commonplace to the subject and everyday things that surround them in their life. In the case of a Western subject, these could be cars, phones, aircraft and so on. Even though the superimposed objects would differ according to culture, the development of the trance state for any given subject would be the same.

In the long-ago past, this faculty was put to far greater use than it is today. In fact, one could say that the more civilized we have become, the deeper within ourselves we have buried this faculty or gift.

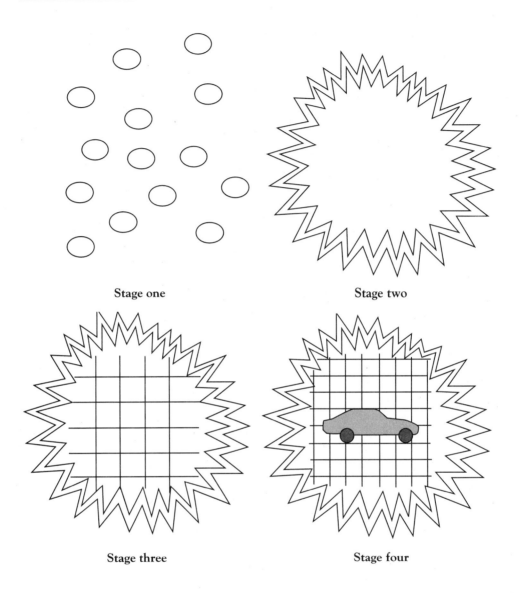

Stage one   Stage two

Stage three   Stage four

Scientific observation of first-state trance has established that the trance-state itself takes on four distinct levels. Each of these levels is marked by a distinctive geometrical pattern effect. Stage one: circles of light against a dark background. Stage two: a flashing irregular zig-zag pattern against a dark background. Stage three: in the center of the zig-zag pattern a grid formation is seen. Stage four: a combination of all three patterns at the same time, while superimposed on the grid formation there appears a series of commonplace articles familiar to the person undergoing the trance experience. The sequence of the trance geometric patterns is common to all humans and is in effect something built into the human nervous system, no matter what race or culture the subject is from.

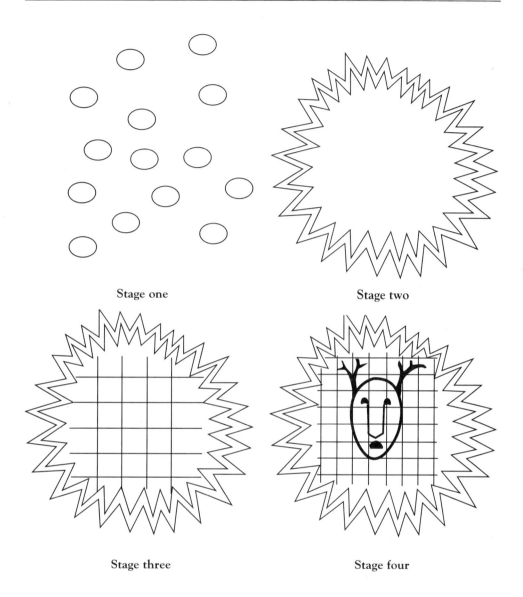

Stage one   Stage two

Stage three   Stage four

As can be seen from the above sketch, the first three sequences of the masked trance working are the same as those of first-state trance. Whereas commonplace articles are usually seen by the trance subject in the final stage, in this case it will be the mask worn for the ritual. In the first stage of the rite, the mask as visualized is an empty mask that gradually as the trance deepens, starts to be endowed with life and instead of being seen just as a mask, slowly changes into the actual animal or bird form. All the time there is the feeling that both the mask and the soul are reaching out to link up with each other. When they do, the soul will be free of the body and ready to reach out beyond this world and cross the river into the world of the spirit.

The mask-and-dance ritual contains within itself the history of the development of human spiritual awareness. It began when we lived as small scattered groups of hunting nomads, using magic to swing the odds of survival. To reach this stage, early people realized that somewhere out there was a force or power that not only created life but also controlled it. Thus would be born the concept of a God or Spirit of the game herds. If this Spirit could be contacted and brought over to the people's side by the use of some form of ritual, then that Spirit would send the bodies of its earthly brothers to where the hunters could kill and eat them. As the concept enlarged and grew in complexity, there also arose the concept of a thanks offering for the kill, plus the realization that the body of the slain animal was also in the form of the Great Spirit that created and then controlled their life and migratory habits. Fanciful? Not when we look at the evidence of carefully stored bones found in the backs of caves as well as the famous antler-headed, hide-draped figures from the Paleolithic cave paintings—those of Les Trois Frères and Le Gabillou in France and from Pin Hole Cave in Derbyshire, for example.

As ancient people created the rites and rituals for aiding the hunt, they would also be reenacting the successful hunt, instructing the younger members of the group in the techniques of hunting. At the same time, they would have also taught the magical spells that ensured the success of the hunt. From this humble beginning grew the concept of the shaman/priest magician in the form of a special servant of the Gods.

If we may extrapolate backward from known hunting cultures, then the first thing the novices had to do, apart from learning the rites, dances, and rituals, was to find the animal-spirit guise by which they would approach the Gods while in a trance state. This would call for them to use all sorts of aids such as starvation, sleep deprivation, certain types of hallucinogens, and pain and suffering, usually through self-mutilation. They aimed to weaken the body's hold on the soul or spirit, and for that spirit to be able to overcome the pain and suffering of the body until it was free to soar away and meet the Godhead, usually in an animal or bird form. Most certainly the path to becoming a shaman was not an easy one, nor was it one that ignored the fact that to gain knowledge one has to suffer, and to gain understanding one must first know pain.

Today this same concept still holds true even if somewhat modified. Very few Witches will disagree with the idea that you can only gain from the Craft by the same amount that you are prepared to put in.

When individual shamans had found their spirit guise or had it settled on them, this would be the mask the soul would assume when in a trance state they journeyed to meet the Gods. The shaman's soul could be sent out by rhythmic dancing, either in that spot or in a circle, a monotonous hypnotic drumbeat setting the pace of the dance, a disorientation of the body to open up the mind—in short, many of the elements to be found in the sacred mask-and-dance tradition of today. The shamanistic rituals were not static, however. As society evolved, so did its religious concepts, and what was once a primitive form of shamanistic spirit worship gradually developed.

In the Mediterranean area, shamanic spiritualism evolved into the classical Gods of both Greece and Rome. In some ways, it could be said that the early Greeks humanized the Gods and Goddesses, while at the same time attributing all the human virtues and vices to them. In northern Europe this spirit worship became a very advanced form of shamanism. Even though religious concepts evolved within the myths of the Nordic Gods, there were still traces of the old shamanistic principles and practices. As a clue to this, one only has to look at the cult of the Vanir and the connection of the Goddess Freya, who according to the sagas was also a priestess of the Vanir. Most certainly, shaman-

istic elements are to be found in the cult of Odin, and at the same time, there is a certain amount of evidence to link Viking worship with Dark Age Anglo-Saxon Wotan worship. Though not absolutely concrete evidence in itself, it certainly points toward a continuity of religious beliefs that finally became known as Anglo-Saxon or English witchcraft.[1] Running through these differing cults is the use of trance state in the worship of the Gods and as a way to determine the will of the Gods.

While there are risks in drawing parallels between different cultures from different times and parts of the world, we may learn something from examining a culture that extends from an equally distant past down to our own age, the so-called Bushmen of southern Africa whose members still practice the rites of their ancestors and are able to interpret the record their ancestors left behind. It was not until there was a concerted effort on the part of South African archeologists to come to grips with examining and cataloging the prehistoric African Bushman rock paintings that they realized just what they had. Not only did they have a widely distributed collection of records of rock art tucked away in the basements of various universities and private collections, there was also a sizable body of evidence concerning the Bushman culture still *in situ*. On top of this, they also had the evidence of the few remaining Bushmen who still understood and were able to follow their ancestors' ways. Furthermore, the descendants of these cave-dwelling Bushmen—now practically wiped out through European-carried diseases, the actions of early white settlers, loss of their environment, and so on—not only understood what these paintings meant, they still perform the same age-old rites today.

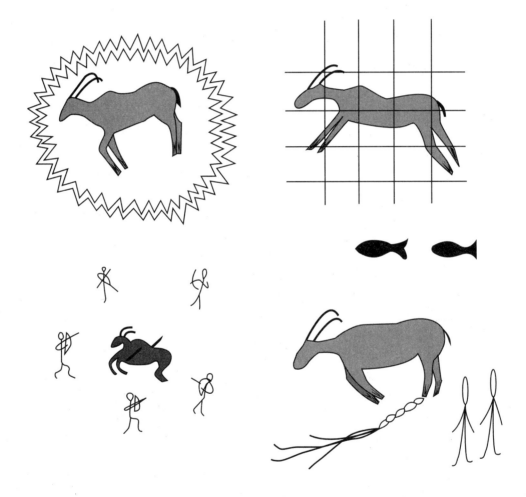

In these illustrations, re-drawn from a selection of Bushman rock paintings, we can see a resemblance to the stages of trance. The rock paintings were not simply works of art, but illustrations of the Bushman technique by which a shaman contacted the tribal spirit in the form of the Great Eland. Although these paintings come from southern Africa, there are enough similarities between them and European rock art to reach a tentative conclusion that the trance-state technique for communicating with the group's totem spirit was common to both cultures, even through the animal totems themselves were different.

Far from being random drawings, the bulk of Bushmen paintings had certain themes running through them. From the earliest known examples to the most modern ones, even though separated by thousands of years, the same themes or patterns occur over and over again. They are now recognized as pictorial representations of a series of concepts concerning the spiritual development of the Bushmen. Interestingly enough, these paintings do not convey their religious concepts in the same way as European religious art does. Instead they portray the methods used to reach out and meet their totem spirit or God. Not until these paintings were examined in closer detail was it realized that in some cases the animal in the picture was superimposed on a faint background. Strangest of all, these selfsame backgrounds corresponded to the geometric patterns first recorded in the American experiments on first-state trance. When photographs of these paintings were shown to present-day Bushmen, they not only recognized them as something coming from their remote ancestors, they also were able to confirm the theory that they illustrated trance-state rituals, the same trance-state rituals being performed by them today.

If we briefly examine the Bushmen's belief, we see that it was centered on the totem spirit of the eland, a large African antelope. The whole culture of these nomadic hunter-gatherers was intertwined with and revolved around the great migratory herds of eland. With their very lives depending on the beast, it was little wonder that the first dawning awareness of some sort of religious expression and belief should center on this animal. To the Bushmen, the Great Eland was the deity that dwelled across the water; in its form of the Dying Eland it was the source of the shamanistic power that could be brought back to this world.

Some of the paintings depict fish, symbolizing the "living dead men who dwelt under the river." It was through them that the spirit of the Dying Eland was contacted. One other point of interest is that some of these paintings show the eland surrounded by men shooting arrows into the animal. There are also representations of one person linked to the arrow-studded dying beast by a chainlike connection springing from the top of his head.

Also, all the figures illustrated have noticeably elongated heads, which according to Bushman lore is where the soul or spirit of the shaman leaves the body to journey across the river to the place where the Great Eland dwells. When the spirit of the traveler returned, it brought back with it some of the life power drained from the dying beast.

When observers witnessed one of their rituals more understanding came. As the ritual progressed and the shaman fell deeper and deeper into a trance state, he began to create the impression of first wading and then swimming in the dust. In effect, the physical body was responding to what the now-absent spirit of the shaman was doing in the trance-state Otherworld. The other dancers not only helped create the atmosphere and conditions for the shaman to leave his body, but they were also on hand to help bring him back to this world again. At one point, the observers felt that the shaman was nearer death than life, and it was the other dancers' constantly lifting him up from the prone position and touching and rubbing his neck and chest that brought him around.

Of all the things that stood out from this rite, the two most noticeable were: first, the state of total disorientation and the speed with which it faded and second, how during this trance state the shaman sweated heavily and his sweat was mopped up by the following and saved on the grounds that some of the power brought back by the shaman was held in this sweat.

When modern practitioners look at this rite, we see all the elements of belief that are to be found in the masked rites to which this book is devoted. We may speculate that in the light of what was discovered about the Bushman culture, closer examination of European rock art shows traces of the same geometric patterns found in the Bushman art. How widespread and common this will turn out to be is unknown. Unlike the South African cave paintings, samples of European cave art are less numerous and do not cover such a long time span. There is enough evidence to reach a tentative conclusion that there was a parallel train of European trance-state development in much the same way as the Bushmen's development of theirs.

In the European case, however, the totem spirit of the group changed with the advent of agriculture. No longer would it be visualized as a somewhat nebulous animal form; instead it would split into two differing forms: one, the male God-figure of the flocks and herds, and the other the Great Earth Mother Goddess (even though in some aspects She would rule over certain animal species). The Great Spirit, ill-defined as it was, was recognized as multi-faceted. Gradually all these faces took on more humanized forms and evolved into distinct Gods and Goddesses in their own right. More and more animal and bird life became associated with and therefore sacred to one particular God or Goddess. So even though humanity had moved on from a purely hunting culture to a life geared to the land and crop growing and even though religious concepts expanded to include this, the basic pathway to the Gods still remained the same.

In our tradition, we too have our pathway, to the Halls of the Goddess (illustrated below). Even though the symbolism is more complex, it still has

This illustration depicts one of the basic concepts of the Old Faith, the journey from the circle to the river and then across to the other side with the pathway to the Hall of the Goddess. Even though the concept is more elaborate and expanded in its symbolism, one basic element still remains that links it to the Bushmen concept illustrated in their rock paintings. The fish often found in the rock paintings symbolizes the river and the living dead men that dwell in the water. Their shaman in spirit form has to cross this river to meet with the spirit of the totem Great Eland, much as the masked dancer medium crosses the river to journey to the Castle of the Pale-Faced Goddess.

within it some of the elements that are found in the Bushman tradition. Perhaps the most telling one of all is the concept of the river between this world and the so-called other side. Instead of swimming the river while in a trance state, we are taken across by the ferryman. This change shows that what is being visualized is the journey the soul must take after death to reach the Castle and Hall of the Goddess, which is the place of waiting for rebirth. Here the soul is washed clean of the last of the old life, while storing the memories of the lessons learned during that life. Much the same way as the Bushmen do, we also realize that there is another way to reach across the barrier—other than in death—to cross the river while in a trance state. Unlike the Bushmen, we do not see the Godhead in animal form akin to the spirit of the Great Eland; we see the Goddess in the form that we were taught to see Her.

In some ways we too are conditioned, for we see the Godhead through the eyes of those who have trodden the selfsame path long before we did. The traditional form that the Godhead takes is one that has been handed down to us as a concrete shape or image of what is in fact an ill-defined, all-embracing formless power. This is so not because we have created the Deity in this image, but because we are human and we can never see the Godhead in totality, only one face or aspect. That face has to take on an image or shape we can comprehend and come to terms with.

The Godhead can be all things to all people. To us, She is the Goddess. In the same way, we have taken the old shamanistic concept of trance workings, shaped it to meet our needs, and now use it as a key to unlock another secret of the mystery that we call the pathway to the Gods. Remember that the faculty to do this is built into each individual, no matter who they are and where they come from. We have not lost the ability to use trance state in the search for the Godhead; all we have done is neglect it.

Notes

1. For more on the shamanistic roots of pre-Christian European religion, see "What Happened to Western Shamanism?" in Chas S. Clifton, ed., *Witchcraft & Shamanism* (St. Paul, MN: Llewellyn Publications, 1994).

Chapter Five

Working the Masked Rites

The masked rites stem from a tradition that lasted longer than the Old Religion itself. In fact, the last living line of masked ceremonial dancers were the medieval mummers with their New Year dances. Frowned on by the Church because of its connection with the Old Religion, this practice was finally suppressed and with its suppression, the final link with our Pagan past was broken.

Our ceremonial use of masks in some ways re-creates the art of the mummer, except that today there is no fully public display of the rite as there was in the past. Although performance of masked rituals at a Pagan festival could be considered "public" in a sense, our usual practice has been to work the rite with only coven members present. Perhaps as time passes modern Pagans will be able to return to something like a masked public drama/display of a magical working, with the true magical and priestly rites worked privately on the eve of the festival.

Throughout the past fifty years of the Craft revival, ours has been seen mainly as a "religion of priests/priestesses." If, however, we do see a situation develop resembling "clergy" and "lay congregations," public masked dramas will indeed become a more prominent part of our religion. Presently, the ceremonial masked rites are done at separate times to the major coven gatherings and these masked rites more or less form a separate gathering within the framework of the coven. We might say that these rites become a mystery within a mystery. How much they are kept apart from the normal workings is purely up to the group concerned. In some covens they are completely divorced from both esbat and sabbat workings.[1] In other cases, masked rites have taken the place of the normal esbat workings and, providing there is no serious magical working to be done, the rites are performed for the sheer pleasure and enjoyment of it. Of course, irrespective of the degree to which the masked rites are integrated into the body of the

Philadelphia Mummers' Museum

The medieval mummers were the last living line of masked ceremonial dancers. Today the elaborately costumed characters are re-created in parades.

coven workings, it must be borne in mind that because of the nature and the differences between the two, there are certain dos and don'ts to be observed.

Fasting and Preparation

Like any other magical working, the masked rites are best preceded with a period of ritual fasting. Fasting facilitates physical and mental preparation for not only ordinary coven workings but especially trance-state rituals. Traditional sources advise total abstinence from food coupled with periods of meditation for the twenty-four hours preceding the rites, but, unfortunately, few people are in a position to do this. For example, if the day before the ritual is spent at an active physical job, some sustenance is necessary. An office worker, on the other hand, could probably abstain from eating with little harm done. It all comes down to a common-sense approach: do not totally give up food if physical harm might result. A person in an air-conditioned office is in a very different situation from, say, a foundry worker or a roofer nailing shingles in the hot sun, for whom salt depletion and faintness could cause serious problems.

At the least, for twenty-four hours you should give up meat, fish, vegetables, alcohol, and salt—unless, like the workers mentioned above, you need to replace the salt lost in perspiration. Toast and boiled eggs would be acceptable, along with tea or coffee, providing, of course, that you follow the basic principle of moderation.

The ritual fast has two purposes. First, it requires willpower, and that same willpower has its magical use within the circle. Second, it helps to train the mind to overlook hunger pangs and the things of the outer world, while focusing the mind's energy on the trance-state working that is to be done. To sharpen the will so that bodily discomforts are ignored and eventually left behind must be looked upon as one of the first steps in separating the soul or spirit from its earthly existence and, in the case of the masked rites, leaving it free to seek out the Godhead.

In the past, the old shaman/priests certainly knew how drugs could be used and most certainly used them to gain the separation effect. The shaman/priest of today uses willpower and willpower alone to reach the same ends and, in effect, becomes a stronger person by doing so.

In the masked workings, the chant, coupled with fasting and breathing control, are the main instruments in bringing about the aimed-at disorientation of the body and the divorcing of the soul from that body. Freed in the form of a pseudo-death, the soul is free

to journey through the Underworld, cross the river of oblivion and gain the halls of the Pale-Faced Goddess, after shape-shifting into the character that the mask being worn portrays. Thus the fast is coupled with the mask to create the aimed-for reality within the illusion of the masked rites.

In our masked workings, unlike regular coven workings, the stang that represents the Horned God/Child presiding over an act of worship to His Mother, the Goddess, is never used. Instead, King Stag, the human representative of the Horned God, carries the wand, which is a miniature version of the stang, as his token of office. Whereas in the coven workings the broom or besom acts as a bridge between the circle and the outside world, King Stag draws each person into the circle in turn by taking their hand as they enter. This act symbolizes the leading of the initiate into the cave/tomb of the mound, the first station on the journey through the Underworld to the dwelling place of the Pale-Faced Goddess.

Unlike the coven ceremonial working worship where the circle can either be a token one or one that is fully charged, the circle for the masked rites is always a fully consecrated one. Because of the nature of the rites, there is always the element of risk that they will be taken over and the leader of the Mill will go into trance. In the masked rites

This 16th-century North American mask probably was worn in re-enactment ritual.

we are dealing with a basic primitive force or power, and there is always a chance that in an unprepared circle, the elemental forces of chaos will leak through. When a person is in trance and wide open to the influences of the Gods, they are also open to the influences of the forces of chaos. To bring these forces into an unprepared circle can be disastrous, not only to the group but to the working site as well. The saying "That out of chaos came order" is one of the basic truths. It was from the primeval chaos that the order of the universe was created, and where the forces of that primeval chaos have

crossed the divide, there is always a sense of evil, making the place feel truly out of harmony and accursed by the very Gods themselves. If this should ever occur, not only will the working site be lost, but the group itself will have to undergo a full rite of purification. In an occult sense, we can say that the elemental spirits of chaos from which the very fabric of the universe was created are still waiting on the fringes of the great void to regain their lost domain.

Beginning the Rite

Groups that have been working together for a long time can use for the masked rites the method they use for consecrating their own coven circle. Others new to the masked rites may feel that because the rites are different from what they are doing now, they would rather have a separate rite of consecration. For them I offer the form that my coven uses.

The consecration is done by King Stag alone (unlike our coven consecration, which in part is done by the lord of the East and the Lady). This tradition recognizes King Stag as the leader of the dance, the sacrificial stag-masked leader of the seven-year reign. He prepares the grave/circle entrance to the Otherworld and the Goddess, and from the inside will reach out to help the others through the portals of

80

the gateway. In many ways, King Stag equates to the Lord of the Mound, keeper of the entrance to the Underworld; thus he is the most logical choice to cast the circle.

If the rite is taking place outdoors, Stag will need two knives, a cord the length of which is a little over half the diameter of the circle being cast, and two small marker posts for forming the northern gateway of the circle. The first thing that Stag does is to drive one of the knives firmly into the ground, establishing the center of the circle. Tying one end of the cord to the hilt and the other end to the second knife, he then determines the north point by using a compass, then, keeping the cord taut, lightly scribes or scratches out the circle, starting at the north. He marks the starting point with one of the marker posts. Stopping a few feet short of making a full circle, he marks the finishing point of the line by the second stake. These two posts form the circle's gateway.

If a fire is to be lit or a lit candle used, then this is the time that it is done. A fire in the center of the circle is optional. Some groups like to use moonlight only, others like a small fire. I have always favored a lit candle in a jar or lantern, as some of the dances take the group away from the circle and the candle acts as a beacon light when finding the way back to the circle again.

With this done, Stag then goes to the gateway of the circle where the others are waiting and helps them into the ring by holding their hand as they jump one by one through the entrance. When all have entered, Stag scribes the final part of the circle between the two markers with his knife, thus closing the gateway to the outer world. The celebrants form a small circle inside the ring.

Consecrating the Circle

Stag must now call upon the four Guardian Spirits of the four quarters, invoking them in the guise of protective deities to safeguard the circle and those within. The first quarter to be invoked is East, realm of the Young Horned King/Child of the May Eve rites, and it is in this aspect that He is called upon as the guardian of that quarter. Going to the East, Stag faces outward and then bows. Next, crossing his arms on his chest, he calls on the God in words like these:

> Lord of the Eastern skies, the incarnate being symbolized by the bright morning star, the Young Horned King, born of fire and clothed in raiments of light from the bright morning, armed with a sword that is the first flashing rays of that sun and darting from the Eastern skies to pierce the

fast-fading night, we call
upon you to stand watch
upon our sacred place, keeping it safe from the forces that
are without. In the name of
the Goddess, we do so ask.

Stag then moves to the Southern
quarter, where once again he faces outward, bows, and crosses his arms, invoking in words such as these:

Our Lady, Goddess of the
night, under whose symbol of
the Moon and by its pale light
we do acts of worship to your
glory, Yours is the pathway of
mystery and hidden things,
and like the dark-haired, soft
and gentle mother that you
are, we ask you to cradle us in
the palm of your hand and
send the shadowy mists of the
night to hide us from the
forces that are to be found
outside this, our sacred place.
In your name, so be it done.

In the West quarter Stag invokes
in words such as these:

Dark lord of the Mound, hooded and cloaked so that none
are able to see your face, we
who stand on the threshold of
your domain do humbly pray
that you will guide our footsteps through the pathways of
your kingdom to the river that
divides this life from the next,

and having crossed this river,
to bring us safely back again to
this sacred place that serves as
a symbolic entrance to your
domain. In the name of the
Goddess, we do so ask.

Finally, Stag goes to the North,
and here once again, as with the other
quarters, he bows and with crossed
arms once again invokes the spirit of
the Goddess only this time in a different aspect:

Pale-Faced Goddess, mistress
and queen of the sacred castle
wherein is found the cauldron
of inspiration, we who have
trodden the path through the
realms of the Underworld to
reach your sacred halls call
upon you once again to keep
shielded our place of worship
from the ever-waiting forces of
chaos that dwell upon the
fringes of order and harmony.
Guide us, we ask thee, to the
place of your cauldron so that
we may partake of the knowledge within it. Then let us,
your servants, tread safely back
along the path to the place
from whence we came. In your
name and by your favor, we do
so ask that this be done.

He then returns to the West, and
for a short while, everyone is silent and
still, letting the atmosphere of the circle and the night envelop them.

Sacred dance begins with a consecrated circle, protected by the four Guardian Spirits.

Choosing a Dance Leader

Now in the West, Stag must turn leadership over to the person who will actually lead the dance. He will pass his wand to the person on his immediate left. It is passed hand-to-hand around the circle until it settles on one person. Which person ends up holding it may be decided in two ways. The first—and one that personally I am rather cautious about—is to pass it hand to hand until one person feels a "call" to claim it, thus making himself or herself leader of the Mill. The potential problem is that one person may be tempted to keep claiming the staff all the time, which defeats the whole aim of the rite. The second method, which I think is preferable, is

for King Stag to close his eyes while the wand is passed from hand to hand round the circle. When Stag feels that the moment is right, he then calls "Stop!" and the person holding the staff is the leader of the Mill.

By using this method, we invoke two ancient and sacred principles. One is that of the Goddess in Her aspect of Blind Fate, and the other, a form of sacred lot. In essence, when lots were once cast or drawn to decide on a person or persons to perform some specific task, it was always believed that the Gods, acting through Blind Fate, would guide the hand of the person selected by them for the task toward the correct token. Most certainly, at one time great religious significance and ritual were attached to drawing lots and seeing in them the will of the Gods. In much the same way, when King Stag calls "Stop!" the Goddess of Fate has placed Her finger on that one person holding the wand at that certain point in time, thereby, in the name of the Gods and by the will of the Gods, selecting the most fitting person to lead the Mill pacing or dance for this one occasion. Archaic though the concept might be, it is still as valid a way as any other because, in effect, the Old Ones are expressing their will through King Stag, priest and leader of the gathering, in the selection of the most fitting person to lead the Mill that is being trodden in their honor.

If, then, the group is using the "blind fate" method, Stag closes his eyes and offers up a silent prayer to the Gods along these lines:

> By closing my eyes, I open up my inner self to the Fates, at whose feet I have placed the selection of a leader for this dance. When they have chosen the one they desire, my inner being will tell me. In the name of the Goddess, so be it done.

If, on the other hand, the Blind Fate method is used, the wand is passed from person to person around the circle until Stag calls "Stop," and whoever is holding the staff at the time is the leader of the Mill or dance. Stag then takes up his new position in the East and just inside the circle. His symbolic role has changed: no longer is he the masked leader of the group. Stag has now become the King of the Castle. The "castle," in this case, is the castle/mound of the grave and King Stag the symbolic representation of the lord of the Mound and the Underworld, looking out at the Following performing a ceremonial rite at the entrance to the grave passage. Only when he has taken up his position in the East will the rest of the gathering be free to tread the Deosil Mill.

The Dance Leader's Role

The person who has the wand now must assume the role of the mask he or she is wearing. I like to begin with a silent prayer like this:

> I am brother/sister to the (naming the mask that is being worn) and call upon the spirit of (naming the animal or bird) to descend upon me and cloak me in its mystic form so that I and the others of this gathering may come to know more fully the nature of the call that has brought each of us to this place of worship. In the name of the Goddess, so be it done.

Now, the person chosen to lead the Mill must create a mental image as well as the feeling that the persona expressed by the mask is gradually wrapping itself around them, and they find themselves looking out at the world through the eyes of that animal or bird. Then and only then will the person be ready to lead off in the pacing of the Mill. Because the Mill is a deosil movement and not widdershins, it will be faster than the pace for a magical one. What is being aimed at is a sense of enjoyment in working the rite, an inward release from tension by divorcing the body from the outside world, and concentrating the whole of one's being to the world of the circle. The duration of the Mill is in the hands of the wand bearer—when they feel the time is right, they stop the Mill.

After everyone has gotten their breath back, Stag leaves his position in the East and rejoins the group. The wand is then passed to the person on the immediate right of the holder and then on around the circle until it reaches Stag again.

Concluding the Rite

The final part of the rite is the sharing of food in the form of token portions of bread and wine. Unlike the coven workings, in this ritual the bread and wine are not consecrated; instead, the bread is regarded as part of a token feast while the wine is looked upon as the cup of fellowship to be shared by all. This sharing of the bread and wine can be as formal or informal as the individuals concerned wish. The only mandatory action is the pouring of a token libation to the Old Gods of both hill and mound and to the Goddess of the high and lonely places. A platter with sufficient pieces of bread on it for all to have one piece is passed around. Stag then proceeds to call down a blessing on the bread:

> With this bread which we
> share we are restating our faith
> that has brought us together
> within this circle. In the same
> way as we have come together
> to do worship to the Old Gods
> and the old ways, so we join
> together in this token sacred
> feast. At this moment in time
> we call upon the Lady, Goddess
> of the night, that by her presence she shall bless this bread,
> making it a sacred token. In
> her name, so be it done.

Then the bread is eaten. Stag fills the cup with wine, and holding it on high, calls upon the Goddess to:

> Bless this cup and the wine
> within, making it worthy
> enough to serve as an offering
> to the Gods. In her name, so
> be it done.

Having said this, Stag then goes to the Eastern quarter. He spills a few drops of the wine on the ground, while at the same time he speaks the words:

In honor of the Young Horned King to whom this libation is offered in a final act of worship. In his name and to his honor, so be it done.

Stag then goes to the Southern quarter where another few drops of wine are spilt, using the words:

In honor of Our Lady, Goddess of the Night, to whom this libation is being offered in our final act of worship. In her name and to her honor so be it done.

Stag then goes to the Western quarter and spills a few more drops, using the words:

In honor of the Lord of the Mound, through whose realm we have passed to reach the

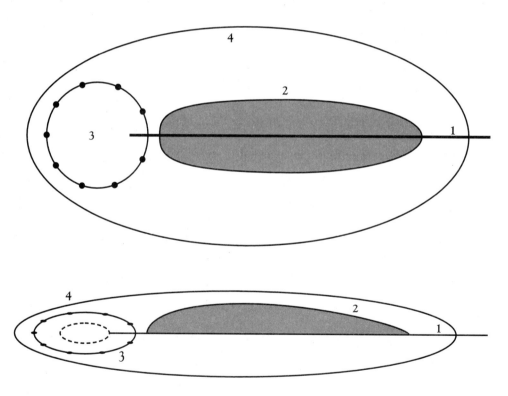

Diagram of a barrow built on sacred ground.

1. Original track
2. Barrow
3. Stone circle.
4. Trench/boundary

river, we pour this libation, token though it may be, in a final act of worship. In his name and to his honor, so be it done.

The final station is the North, where all the wine left in the cup is emptied on the ground while Stag says:

In honor of the Pale-Faced Goddess of the North, in whose halls we hope one day to dwell while awaiting the time of rebirth into this world, where once again we shall know and live a life span putting to use the things that we have learned in this life. From this cup now empty we have poured the last libation in a final act of worship. In the name of the Goddess and to Her honor, so be it done.

With the cup now emptied, Stag returns to the gathering and fills it once again. Once more he lifts the cup on high, calling on the Goddess:

Once more we call upon You to charge this cup as a blessing, so that all who partake of it in fellowship will at the same time partake of Your blessing. In our Lady's name, so be it done.

Stag then passes it to the person on his immediate left, who takes a token sip and passes it on to the next person. In each case, it is only a token wetting of the lips that is observed, because the cup once filled in the name of the Goddess and fellowship and blessed by Her can never be refilled at this meeting. Each must share in it, while at the same time leaving some for the others. Any wine that is left after the cup has been passed around is swallowed by Stag, who then turns the cup upside-down to prove that it is empty, while at the same time saying:

The wine is finished, the cup now empty, the rite is done. As we came into the circle, so shall we leave it. In the name of the Goddess and the Old Gods, so shall it be done.

When everyone has left the circle by jumping across the line between the two markers, Stag pulls the markers up and then throws them away. By doing this, Stag in effect is letting anything raised within the circle drain away back to earth.

The illustration of an ancient barrows on page 86 helps in understanding the masked ceremonial rites. It is drawn from an actual recorded dig, at Crickley Hill, just outside Cheltenham, Gloucestershire, which dates back to at least 3200 B.C.E. The earliest known structure on the site was a small wooden nemeton.[2] Much later on, this site and the track leading to it was overlaid by a long barrow with a stone circle located at the western end of it and replacing the wooden structure. Surrounding the site is a shallow trench. The interesting thing is that except for one point where traces of a screen have been found, the only place where anyone can see the whole of the site is from inside the trench. On this evidence, it is a pretty fair assumption that the rites held here would have only been witnessed by those who were invited to take their place within the trench/ boundary. What we are looking at is a particular place set apart for a special form of rite connected to the dead and their resting place. Also, it was not the barrow that made the place special, it was because the area was considered sacred that the barrow was built where it was.

To claim that our ceremonial rites as written down are direct descendants from the rites once done in the stone circle would of course be blatantly false, but we may say that in both ceremonial and magical masked workings the circle we cast represents the circle at the entrance to the grave/mound passage to the Underworld. When we look at the barrow and circle layout, we are looking at the symbolic layout that should be created mentally when setting up the site for a ceremonial working. In the same light, when Stag takes his position in the East, he would be standing at the entrance of the symbolic barrow passage/gateway that leads to the Underworld and looking out at the rite being performed. In the same way, the disembodied spirit of the trance dancer would use the symbol of the barrow and Stag as the keeper of the gateway at the entrance to the Underworld and the river.

Notes

1. In much of British Traditional Witchcraft, *sabbat* denotes a festive seasonal meeting, and *esbat* a "working" meeting, determined by the lunar calendar.

2. Roman writers used the word *nemeton* to describe shrines set in sacred groves where the Celtic peoples of Europe worshiped. Here the term is used loosely for a much older wooden shrine. For more information on ancient British ritual sites, see Ronald Hutton, *The Pagan Religions of the Ancient British Isles* (Oxford: Blackwell, 1991).

Chapter Six

The Dances of the Following

We begin with Raven's ritual dance because it is the most complicated one of all. It is the only rite that involves leaving the circle and taking the ritual into another area. Two distinct levels of involvement have to be understood before the thing makes any sense at all. On one level Raven is the trickster, and in this guise has to create a magical illusion within the minds of the people taking part. Raven must create an imaginary journey that takes the dancer from the circle into a magical maze, to the visionary tower of enchantment, and then back out again.

The Dance of Raven

Raven's rite requires divorcing the inner being from the body through breathing control, chanting, and the pacing of the magical maze. In the past, of course, this would have been a far easier proposition because the maze path would have been laid out as part of a sacred site. Today this is not likely, so there has to be an improvised version of the maze dance.

In one form, Raven can take the dancers into a decreasing spiral dance, using a candle lantern as the central point that is to be worked toward and then finishing off with a Mill working around the lantern—the same way as the Mill is trodden around the fire in coven workings. When it is time to leave the place, an ever-widening reverse spiral is paced, leading back to the starting point on the edge of the circle.

In the other form, Raven tries to create the feeling of treading the maze by using a twisting, turning, seemingly random path that will end with the Mill being trodden around a lantern. When the dancers leave this spot, another random pattern path is trodden leading back to the circle.

Both patterns mimic in the physical plane a magical journey to the enchanted tower that lies between the spirit world of the Gods and the physical world of the dancer. The world of dreams and visions intertwines with fact and reality to create the dream-state Otherworld where illusion and reality become one and the same thing. Raven's task is to create through chanting and movement the atmosphere for the magical journey of the mind and spirit, while at the same time taking the physical bodies of the dancers through an actual journey.

The next thing to look at is laying out of the site for the working of the Raven ritual. The accompanying illustration (page 91) presents an idealized version of the concept. Notice that in addition to the ritual circle, a second area is marked out by thirteen wands, ideally cut from hazel wood. This second area will be declared sacred to the Gods for a magical reason. As the illustration shows, the circle's perimeter is broken by what will become the western gateway. During Raven's dance, the dancers leave the circle by this opening and work the spiral or maze dance in this area.

The previous chapter discussed how the ritual circle forms a barrier against the chaotic forces that are on the outside. The same conditions exist for this rite. Unless the area to be entered is protected, the dancers would be wide open to the ever-present forces of chaos when they leave the circle. Therefore we consecrate this second area, dedicating it to the Gods in much the same way as the old Celtic nemeton was dedicated. The thirteen wands symbolize the wooden stockade that in ancient times would have been erected around the nemeton. Once the wands are placed in position and the ground consecrated, the area then becomes *de facto* a sacred site just as it did in the past.

In using peeled hazel wands rather than any old stick, we invoke the ancient magical tradition that certain

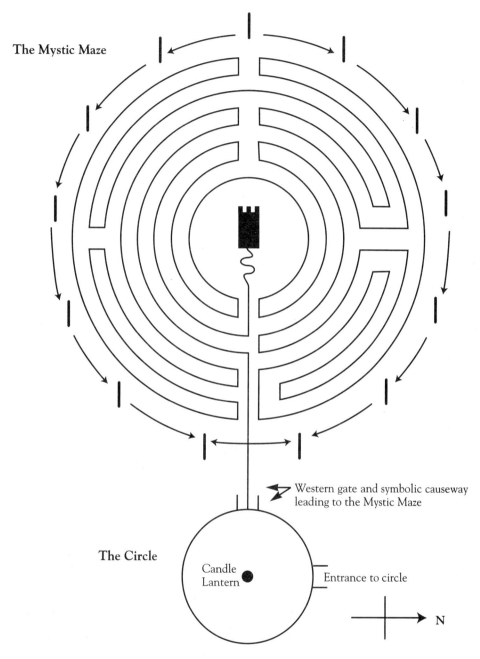

The Mystic Maze

Western gate and symbolic causeway leading to the Mystic Maze

The Circle

Candle Lantern

Entrance to circle

N

This idealistic portrayal of the concept behind the Raven rite may be followed in laying out the site for the working of the Raven ritual. The Enchanted Tower is found at the center of the Mystic Maze. Thirteen hazel wands mark out the sacred area.

trees have specific magical meanings. In the language and lore of the trees, the hazel's attributes have always included wisdom, divination, and knowledge. These are the things we are trying to gain through journeying to the mystic tower. On a more prosaic level, peeling the wands before they are placed in position leaves them nice and white. One thing that is noticeable when working out in the open at night is how quickly everyone develops night vision. Because the candle lantern gives out only a fairly low level of light, it does not impair this night vision too much. Thus the dancers will see the wands and stay within the marked area.

It is a good idea is to inspect the ritual site in the daylight to give everyone a chance to look at the lay of the land and select the flattest part for what will become an open-air temple to the Gods. If possible, bring the hazel wands then, peel them, and place them in position. Providing they are not disturbed, the area will be consecrated later that night. Anything that makes the preparation of the site easier should be more than welcome; planting thirteen hazel wands in the dark to form a sacred area is not a simple task.

When the circle is cast for the start of the rite, the western gate is in fact always opposite the sacred area, which is always to the west of the gateway. How far apart they are is not all that important. As the wording of the rite will later show, the distance between the two is symbolic of the sacred or ritual causeway, the remains of which have been found at many sites.

© Malcolm Brenner / Eyes Open

Raven leads the dancers through mazes such as this one shown above.

Apart from the usual tools and wands needed to scribe out the circle and mark the northern entrance, the Raven rites require two extra marker wands for the western gate, plus a small bag of salt for use in consecrating the sanctuary area. Casting the circle for the Raven rites differs very little from the casting of the normal working circle. Stag marks the center of the circle with a knife driven firmly into the ground. and proceeds in the manner described in the previous chapter, but when he reaches the western point of the circle while scribing it with his knife, he plants the two marker posts. Stag goes on to finish scribing the circle in the usual way.

Stag then brings everyone into the circle and closes the northern gate. Using the same prayers as are used in the ceremonial circle to invoke the Guardians of the four quarters, Stag then calls on each of them in turn, starting in the East and finishing up in the North. Instead of joining the others as he usually does at the center of the circle, Stag now goes to the western gate, which must be ritually activated and brought under the protection of a guardian deity. Because of the nature of the area, the divinity invoked as the guardian of the gate should have recognizable powers as a protecting spirit. We call upon the old God of the crossroads, Myrddin, lord of the high and lonely

Evan John Jones

Stag mask made from papier mâché.

track ways, to protect the gateway. The pathway the dancers are going to take crosses the power line—the edge of the circle. Thus, in effect, we have a crossing of the ways, appropriate for Myrddin. Invoking Myrddin taps into a stratum of mystic experience and expression that is not only native to our land, but part of our blood and race inheritance as well.

The invocation also includes the Goddess Elen and Her sacred causeway. Elen is the Goddess of the old arrow-straight military road, and reputed Goddess of the war bands, a connection commemorated in certain old roads and tracks still known as *Ffordd Elen* (Elen's road) or *Sarn Elen* (Elen's causeway). What better spirit to invoke as protection for the short path between the circle and the sacred site that the old Goddess of the causeway Herself?

At the time of consecration, Stag goes to the western gate and after a few moments of silence, goes down on one knee and strikes the ground sharply with the butt end of his staff three times to summon the God. Having done this, he then stands up with his right arm extended and horizontal to the ground, with the horns of the wand pointing toward the opening of the gateway. He then calls on the old God using words like these:

I call on Myrddin, lord of the old crossways, guardian of where the four ways meet, calling on Your name by the right of the office that I hold, to lend us Your presence and Your power to keep safe this gateway between our circle and the place beyond, where we shall journey in search of the old knowledge as others have done in the past. Because our way shall take us beyond the safety of our magic circle where harm shall come to none, hold back, we pray, with all Your cunning and all Your Power the forces of chaos that lie in wait along the fringes of existence, ready and waiting to bring chaos and destruction to where harmony and balance

now reign. We also call on Elen, Goddess of the old causeway, to keep safe our steps and guide them as we cross the Sarn Elen to the sanctuary of the old beloved Gods. Her presence and Her spirit we do so invoke. All this we do in the name of the Goddess, She who is as time itself, the nameless formless One whose only visible sign of Her coming and Her presence that is shown to man is the white owl. In Her name it is so asked, and in Her name, so be it done.

Once again Stag goes down on one knee and strikes the ground sharply three times with the butt end of the hand staff.

Next, Stag crosses what is now considered to be the sacred causeway and enters the area enclosed by the thirteen hazel wands. Assuming the center of this is going to be marked by a candle lantern, Stag will bring it with him and place it in the chosen spot before starting the rite of cleansing and consecration. In many ways, this follows the general pattern of rite used for dealing with the February circle in the coven Candlemas rites. This time, instead of the lady doing them, it will be Stag who with the bag of salt first goes to the eastern quarter and scatters a little of the salt around, while at the same time saying:

With this salt I banish all that has gone on in this place before. As in the past our ancestors once sowed a site with salt wherein no man dare dwell, thus I do likewise. With this salt I do dedicate this place to the Mother, our Lady, the Goddess of the three faces and in Her name do declare this place to be sacred.

This time Stag touches the ground three times with the horned end of the wand before going next to the South, then to the West and finally to the North, repeating his words and actions at each quarter. He then returns to the center of the area where, if there is any salt left, he scatters it broadcast, saying:

The salt is scattered, the site now cleansed and dedicated to the Old Gods. With the opening of the gateway and the making sacred of the causeway thus forming in total a shrine and sanctuary to the Mother from whence we Her servants shall gain some of Her wisdom and Her understanding, now let the Raven rite begin.

Stag then returns to the circle where the others are awaiting him. After a few moments of silence, Stag passes the horned wand to the person on his immediate left, who passes it around the gathering until it reaches Raven, who on taking it then becomes the leader of the ritual.

When Raven feels the time is right, he or she will step outward away from the others and start to pace a solitary widdershins Mill while chanting the song or chant of Raven (see below). This chant sets the pace of the Mill. The responses of the rest of the group in chorus set in motion the changes in body chemistry that bring about the trance-state, divorcing of the soul from the body. Raven, by being the first one to start the Mill, gives the others of the group time to settle into the pace of the Mill while getting the feel of the chant and the way it relates to the speed of the pace. When Raven instinctively feels that the time is right, she or he touches Stag on the shoulder as they are pacing around the circle, a signal for the rest of the group to follow Stag and Raven into the widdershins Mill.

This movement is kept up until Raven instinctively feels that it is now time to leave the circle, cross the causeway, and enter the shrine of the Gods, using either the spiral or the random maze pattern dance. Raven's chant and the group's chorus should continue because it is nothing more than a form of mantra used to occupy both mind and body, letting the spirit soar free. This "EEE...AAA...III...OOO" chant is always a long, drawn-out, deep-pitched, resonant one.

The Chant of Raven

RAVEN: I am Raven, taker of souls that have lived their span, leading them away to the hidden land.

GROUP: EEE...AAA...III...OOO (The group repeats the mantra-like vowel chant after each of Raven's following lines.)

RAVEN: Give me your trust and give me your hand, and I shall lead you to this hidden land.

GROUP: EEE...AAA...III...OOO Round and round we shall go, stepping together with a pace that is so slow.

Outward and onward down the twisting track, magic circle to our back.

Between the trees we wend our way, our only light the pale Moon's rays.

Deeper and deeper as though in a trance, with Will-o-the-Wisp now leading the dance.

I am Raven, and only I know where to go with a pace that is steady and yet so slow.

Pacing onward and inward through the night, searching for a glimpse of light.

That burning steady and burning bright will lead us to the hidden site.

Fire of knowledge and rebirth pain is the price we pay once again.

As we tread the hidden Mill, on this night so quiet and still.

So pace the circle and tread the Mill, while the Gods our minds do fill.

To the mystic tower we must go, where She to us Her wisdom will show.

When the rite is done and power wanes, then Raven will lead you back again.

The twisting path you I shall show, for I am Raven and I know.

Back to the place that we all know, along the twisting path we go.

For I am Raven, the one who knows.

With this chant, leading the group through either the inward spiral or the random maze dance, Raven would now have brought the group to the area where the candle lantern acts as a center point of the site. Here, the gathering has a choice of previously decided-upon working methods. They may decide that they are going to work the widdershins Mill around the lantern while continuing Raven's Chant and just let anything that is coming through from the other side sink in individually. Alternatively, Raven may lead everyone into the Mill and then after a short period of working the Mill, fall silent and move slightly out and away from the others. They carry on doing the widdershins Mill in silence while Raven starts doing a deosil or counter-Mill around them, about four or five feet out from the others. This movement symbolizes Raven pacing round the inside wall of the mystic tower and setting its bounds. By doing this and working in silence, the group can imagine they are now inside the "Mystic Tower of Enchantment" working their Mill.

Given time and constant practice by working together, the group will in time start to create a shadowy impression of the actual tower. It may be vague and half-formed, but it will still be there because it is what the eye wishes to see and the mind is conditioned to see. Illusion, yes, a magical illusion that has to a certain degree become a reality, but the instinctive feelings and knowledge that come flooding through while working in this illusory tower are not illusion or a figment of anyone's imagination. All those present will feel and understand this, while one person alone will be chosen and used as the vehicle for passing back the knowledge and

understanding gained from working, irrespective of the version of the Mill being used. It is up to Raven to decide the length of the ceremony. Only when Raven calls "Stop" will the group cease to work the Raven Mill.

Having halted the proceedings, Raven will allow three or four minutes of silence for people to get their breath back again before speaking. Raven then speaks in words such as these:

> As father of both thought and memory I command you all to carry back in your minds the memory of all that has taken place. For what has been given to us on this night is the gift of the Goddess Herself. By bearing this away within your minds the gift of thought can be brought to bear upon it, seeking to find the best meaning and way to use what we have been given, to improve our understanding of what we are and why we do what we do. By Her grace and in Her name, so be it done.

Having spoken the final words of the ritual, Raven now winds the rite down. Instead of leading everyone off into a widdershins Mill again, Raven starts pacing a deosil Mill, leading the group around a few times before either using an outwardly spiraling pacing or dance, or the same random maze pattern again. Raven's Chant should be repeated to set the pace and speed, exactly as was done on the journey to the sacred site. The return to the circle is more or less a repeat of the leaving of it. When everyone has formed the circle in the middle of the magical ring around the candle lantern and has stopped, Raven will do a few more circuits of the deosil Mill before stopping and joining the others around the lantern.

Once again there is a short pause before Raven silently returns the hand staff to Stag by passing it to the person on his or her immediate left, who passes it on around the circle until it reaches Stag.

Stag takes it, steps back from the circle of participants, and begins the rite's ending. First he closes the gateway to the West by removing the twin markers, and then uses the butt of the wand to trace a line across where the opening was. Even though in itself this is a token act, it does seal the circle off once again from the causeway and the sacred area beyond. Unlike the ceremonial rites where there is a token feast held within the circle, in the rite of Raven, there is no feast. All that Stag does is pour a libation to the old God Myrddin and the Goddess of the causeway, Elen, in the West. First filling the cup with wine and then

holding it aloft, Stag calls upon the Goddess to:

> Bless this cup and the wine within, making it worthy enough to serve as an offering to the Gods. In Your name, Lady, so be it done.

Stag then goes next to the Eastern quarter and spills a few drops of wine on the ground, while saying:

> To the honor of the Young Horned King, to whom this libation is being offered, a final act of worship in His name and to His honor. So be it done.

Stag repeats the libation at the South, saying:

> In honor of our Goddess of the Night, to whom this libation is being offered in a final act of worship. In Her name and to Her honor, so be it done.

On going to the Western quarter, Stag pours a small libation to the Lord of the Mound, using the words:

> In honor of the Lord of the Mound, to whom this libation is being offered in final act of worship. In His name and to His honor, so be it done.

Stag then pours a second libation in the West to honor Myrddin and the Goddess Elen, saying:

> Myrddin, lord of the old cross-ways, where once in the past others have offered a libation to you at the end of their journey, we now do so again as a thanks offering for Your protection on our journey from the circle. At the same time, we also offer this libation and our thanks to the Goddess Elen for keeping safe the causeway that we used to reach the place beyond the circle. In the name of the Goddess and the Old God, thus we have so done in part payment of our debt.

Stag then moves to the North where all the wine left in the cup is poured in honor of the Goddess, using the words:

> To honor the Pale-Faced Goddess of the North, in whose halls we hope some day to dwell while awaiting the time of rebirth, where once again we shall know and live a life-span putting to use the things that we have learned in this one. From this cup now emptied we have poured the last libation as a final act of worship. In the name of the Goddess, so be it done.

After pouring the last of the wine on the ground, Stag stays in the North ready to help the others out of the circle, one by one. When all are out, with the last one to leave bringing with them the candle lantern, Stag then pulls up the two northern markers. Only then will Stag go around the shrine area, remove the thirteen hazel wands, and retrieve the lantern left behind by the group when they returned to the circle.

After this, if the members so feel, there can be a gathering away from the site, in someone's house or in a suitable outdoor place, to let off a bit of steam and talk things over. Have a few drinks and laughs by all means, because this is one way of earthing the ritual and bringing everything back to normal.

At this point, you must understand one thing clearly. In order to keep the flow of the written version of the rites going, the actions and techniques used by the group when dealing with someone in trance-state, and how they are helped back to this plane, have been left out. Remember that the whole reason for doing these rites is to bring about a trance state. It then becomes the duty of the group to help return again to this world whomever it is that has gone over. Because this can and, indeed, should happen at any time during the rite, I think it would be better dealt with under a separate heading later on in the book. In all cases of trance state, the technique for dealing with it and helping the subject back to this world is the same. Doing this must be a part of any group training and should be understood by all before any trance-state workings are ever attempted.

The Dance of Squirrel

Although this is another of the formal rituals, the rite or dance of Squirrel is far less complex than that of the Raven. Instead of being spread out between two working sites, it is confined to the one magical circle. On the other hand, it is more shamanistic, perhaps the most so of all the dances of the Following. Of all the masks in the gathering, no matter what sex Squirrel is, the one ability they must have is the faculty of being a trance medium. I use "trance medium" in the old meaning of the word, rather than in the modern sense of sitting around a table holding hands and waiting while in a trance state for messages to come through from the "Other Side." The mediumship of Squirrel is far more active than this, for it stems from a far older tradition of magical working and experience, one that is perhaps the most universally accepted concept of the priestly messenger to the Gods.

To really get into the spirit of the concept and role of Squirrel within the rites, look at the creature itself and translate this into cult-oriented symbols and terms. Squirrels are tree dwellers, and the sheer speed with which they can move up and down the trunk and out along the branches of a tree is amazing, and also a pleasure to watch. In the Nordic concept of the World Tree "Yggdrasill," the tree that stretches from its roots which are in the Underworld, with its trunk passing through this world, and with its upper branches in the heavens, it is easy to see how Squirrel, a freely moving tree-dweller, would come to represent the shamanistic spirit of the medium that, once freed from the body, is able to move up and down the tree, using it as a ladder between the three worlds.

This ability recalls the old tradition of shape-shifting. Indeed, when Squirrel starts the rite, they transform their soul or spirit into the shape of the Squirrel which has the ability to run up and down the World Tree as the bearer of messages between this world, the Underworld, and the Heavens, becoming the divinatory priest or priestess of the rites. Writing nearly three centuries after the official conversion of Iceland to Christianity, the Icelandic author Snorri Sturlsson described how in Norse mythology, "A squirrel, by name Ratatoskr, darts up and down about the tree [Yggdrasill] bearing spiteful tales between the eagle and Níohöggr." Despite the connotation Snorri Sturlsson may have added, the idea of Squirrel as a shamanic traveler remains, for the eagle, "wise beyond all knowing," roosts in the high realm of the Gods while Níohöggr, "the Biter," is the Underworld dragon who perpetually gnaws at Yggrasill's roots.[2]

Another of Squirrel's links is to the old Nordic tradition of *seithr* witchcraft and to the Goddess Freya who, according to the sagas, was Herself a priestess of the Vanir cult of which *seithr* witchcraft was one part. The priestess, or *volva*, would sit on a high wooden tower while other people at its foot sang and chanted the spells that brought about a state of ecstasy. Then she would answer questions put to her by the following.

Another example of this type of ecstasy comes from an Irish account of a Viking raid on the great monastery of Clonmacnoise. A woman named Aud, wife of a Norwegian Viking, went into a mediumistic trance while seated on the church's high altar, much to the offense of the Irish monks.[3]

Whereas the Norse *volva* was female, Squirrel today may be male or female, as long as she or he possesses a talent for divination and mediumship. It is this aspect of Squirrel that makes this one rite a highly individual one, shaped more by the person than anyone else. The rest of the group's main function is to provide the keys for Squirrel to slip into the prophetic trance-state that lets the soul go forth to meet the Gods.

I do not, therefore, advocate recreating the role of the *volva* priestess

Jeff Farnam

The enthusiasm of these dancers is evident as they dance along the parade route.

and calling it the rite of Squirrel. What was done in the past should stay firmly locked in the past and should only be looked to as an aid to determining how the modern-day Squirrel will act within the modern-day rites. For this is what has to be done: the role of Squirrel has to be defined in the way that the group would like to see the role interpreted.

Approaches to carrying out the rite of Squirrel vary. Some people prefer that Squirrel join in the working of the Mill and then chant him- or herself into first-state trance. Others think that Squirrel does a solitary Mill either inside or outside a ring formed by the other members while they chant the spell of the Squirrel, sending him or her into the trance-state. Another view is that Squirrel stands still while the others of the gathering tread the Mill around her or him while chanting, using this to send Squirrel into the trance.

For myself, I would not like to claim that one way is better than another; it all depends on the personality of the person acting as the Squirrel. Whatever way suits them or that they feel right with is the best, or perhaps the only way for them to work. All I can do is write/tell how I have seen it done and then let people make up their own minds and perhaps use what has been written here as a guide to forming their own Squirrel way or path.

Following the procedure that is normal for all the masked workings, Stag will first cast and then consecrate the circle. He will then bring everyone into it and, finally, close it. Having invoked the Guardians of the four quarters, he then joins the others in the center of the circle. He allows a few moments of silence before speaking the opening words of the rite:

Once more we are gathered within the bounds of this our circle. Our aim is to reach out beyond the limits of this world through our brother [sister], the Squirrel. As was done in the past, we now so do again today. For in this reaching out by one of us, the knowledge and wisdom thus gained is shared by the many doing this. We make ourselves as one with the spirit of the land, thus once again taking our rightful place within the natural order of things. The Spirit of Creation that first brought order out of chaos and gave form to this, our universe, is still with us and waiting for us to reach out beyond our present selves to where the Goddess dwells. In Her name, so be it done.

There is another pause for a minute or so, and then Stag moves slightly outward and away from the others and walks around the gathering until he reaches Squirrel. Tapping Squirrel on the right shoulder with the horns of the wand of office, he then says:

> By touch of the symbol of the
> Horned God, the powers that
> I hold now pass to you. For
> this rite is your rite and
> belongs to no other. In this,
> you are the instrument of the
> Goddess. Through you, the
> secret wisdom of the Old Ones
> shall flow to us, the congrega-
> tion. In Her name and by Her
> willing joining, so be it done.

Tapping Squirrel on the shoulder three times with the wand, Stag then says:

> From me to thee the powers of
> office and leadership have
> now been passed. So be it now
> done.

Once again, it must be stressed that what is described here is only one of the ways of working the Squirrel rites. Individual groups will have to experiment with the form their rites will take before deciding how they will finally work them. In this particular case, Stag takes up his usual position in the North, just inside the perimeter of the circle, with the other members doing the same and spreading themselves around the edge of the circle. Squirrel then starts the deosil Mill at a slow pace while letting his or her mind go empty. Very often the rest of the gathering will help to create the atmosphere needed for the Squirrel-seer to cross over the boundary between this world and the psychic world by chanting something along the lines of:

> Four states of being you
>   shall know,
> Yet to only three you can go.
> To Abred where all life began,
> To Gwynfid where all have
>   transcended sin,
> Then to Annwn where the
>   damned souls go.
> All these places you must
>   know.
> And to all these places you
>   must go.

This is repeated over and over again by the Following, while at the same time they gently clap their hands in unison to create the timing and the pace of both the Mill and the chant. Of course, a group could make up its own chant or even use no chant at all, only a solitary drumbeat, to set the pace of the Squirrel mill. All the chants serve to help bring about the disorientation and changes in the body chemistry of the Squirrel-seer that are needed for the soul or spirit of Squirrel to shape-shift into its animistic form and then run up and down the World Tree seeking knowledge and understanding from both the Underworld and the world of "Enlightened Souls."

Meanwhile, Stag must keep a careful eye on Squirrel during the Mill. At some time during the rite Squirrel will start picking up the pace of the Mill, her (or his) stride getting longer and longer, so that instead of pacing the Mill, she will in fact start leaping or bounding around the circle, flapping her arms as though they were wings. From personal observation, feeling, and memory, I can attest that just before crossing over when everything becomes a total blank, Squirrel will have the sensation of almost being able to fly.

After this point has been reached and passed, one of two things will happen. Either Squirrel will just simply fold up and flop on the ground, or will start to stagger around aimlessly. In the latter case, Stag and one or two of the others will make Squirrel sit down before questions are put to him or her by Stag. After the questions have been put to them and answers given, Squirrel is then brought back to this world in a way that will be dealt with later on in this book.

Once back to this world and somewhat recovered, Squirrel is questioned once again on what she or he has seen, heard, and experienced. In many cases, after the Squirrel spirit has regained the body, he or she will be subject for several hours to intense "elevated" or anagogic feelings that gradually fade. During this stage Squirrel will suffer paramnesia and it then becomes the job of the group to sort out the true from the false memories by recalling what was asked and said while Squirrel was in the first-state trance.

In the second method of working, instead of Squirrel being the one who paces the mill, he or she takes their place in the center of the circle, usually seated on a low stool, after the opening part of the rite has been performed by Stag. The rest of the members start to pace a deosil Mill around Squirrel, keeping to the usual slow, steady pace while at the same time fitting the flow and rhythm of the chant to the pace of the Mill. Squirrel then has to let his or her mind empty on a conscious level while simultaneously conjuring up his or her spirit-animal shape, letting it come to the fore and gradually blend in with his or her own. At the same time, Squirrel will have to make the conscious and deliberate effort to control their breathing by using the pace of the Mill as a measure to time it by. In some ways, the effort of doing this serves to focus the conscious mind long enough for the animistic spirit to meld with the soul of the person, and then for both to soar free of the body and start the spiral journey up and down the World Tree.

Personally, I have always had the feeling that this method is the least satisfactory way of all. It leaves Squirrel with a lot to do, without involving him or her in the physical effort needed to pace the Mill that in many ways is the key to the body changes needed to bring about the disorienting of the body and the subsequent releasing of the soul for the start of its journey. For this method of working, Squirrel would have to be well versed in techniques of meditation and self-trance inducement, because with the rest of the group pacing around, their activity becomes less an aid to the creation of the atmosphere needed and more something going on in the background that Squirrel will in time have to ignore.

All in all, working this way depends a lot on the ability of Squirrel as the medium/seer of the group to send her- or himself on the journey. That task is less group-managed and one that depends on the ability of Squirrel to do it in a more passive and unaided way. Yet having said this, when I have seen this way being worked, the results were excellent, mainly because the Squirrel dancer was an exceptional one and because the group had been working together for a long time.

Yet another way that I have seen the Squirrel rites worked was as a guest of an old, established group working just outside Oxford. In this particular case, the rite was an extremely formal one

and strangely enough, it was the only time I had ever seen or heard of where the coven stang was ever used in the masked rites. Each participant brought along his or her own personal stang. When Stag had brought the participants into the circle, before going to the center, each person planted a stang in the ground just inside the circle's edge, until there was a second circle of stangs around the inside. Stag then planted the coven stang firmly in the center of the circle, and Squirrel then sat down against it, facing the North.

At the start of the rite, everyone went to where their stang was planted and stood in front of it in dead silence. Squirrel then started the chant, and at a nod from Stag, the rhythm was taken up by one person on a small drum. The beat being tapped out by the drummer was of four beats with the first one the loudest and the subsequent three distinctly quieter—all at a steady, regular, and semi-hypnotic monotonous beat. All the time this was going on, Squirrel was matching the words of the chant with the tempo of the drum. After a while, Squirrel stopped chanting and started describing the journey being taken.

At this point, the questions were put and answers given. How relevant this was to what the group was seeking, I would not like to say, not being a member of this particular group. I can say, however, that what I saw was not only impressive, it also had the feeling of a genuine occurrence about it. Above all the rite possessed that rather special atmosphere that one feels in the presence of a genuine magical working.

When I eventually asked why, unlike other groups, they brought the coven stang into the circle, and what it meant, I was more or less told that if I couldn't work out what it symbolized, then what the hell was I doing in a Witches' circle in the first place, and to go away and think about it for a while and to come back when I had an answer.

This I did, and the answer was so blatantly obvious that I could have kicked myself for not knowing it. The people concerned also confirmed that what I had come up with matched what they saw as being symbolized by placing the stang in the center of the circle.

After Squirrel has regained a state of equilibrium, it is then the job of Stag to close the rite down with the pouring of the token libation at each of the quarters as a thanks-offering to the four guardian spirits or aspects. This closing follows the same pattern as given above in the rite of Raven. Stag fills a cup, blesses it, and, beginning at the East, pours out a little at each quarter before emptying the cup at the North.

(Blessing) Bless this cup and the wine within, making it

worthy enough to serve as an offering to the Gods. In Your name, Lady, so be it done.

(East) To the honor of the Young Horned King, to whom this libation is being offered, a final act of worship. In His name and to His honor, so be it done.

(South) In honor of our Goddess of the night to whom this libation is being offered in a final act of worship. In Her name and to Her honor, so be it done.

(West) In honor of the Lord of the Mound, to whom this libation is being offered in final act of worship. In His name and to His honor, so be it done.

(North) To honor the Pale-Faced Goddess of the North, in whose halls we hope some day to dwell while awaiting the time of rebirth, where once again we shall know and live a lifespan putting to use the things that we have learned in this one. From this cup now emptied we have poured the last libation as a final act of worship. In the name of the Goddess, so be it done.

Finally Stag helps everyone out of the circle, and then he pulls out the two markers, either throwing them away or taking them with him for later use.

After the Squirrel ritual there must be some sort of formal or informal gathering. Squirrel and perhaps some of the other members will be subject to a certain amount of anagogic feeling that must be talked out of them. In addition, very often Squirrel will go over what has happened during the working in his or her mind.

Without a doubt, at this stage there will be certain false memories of what went on and what was seen, because of the group knowing what has been asked while Squirrel was in a trance. These false memories can and should be separated from the true ones as part of the general unwinding that should bring everyone back to a more stable emotional level.

One of the drawbacks to any sort of serious magical working is that a heightened emotional atmosphere is generated which has to be brought down to earth. Performing Squirrel's rite tends to produce this atmosphere more strongly than do many others, and unless it is "earthed," these heightened emotions can be carried over into normal life, where they may play havoc with a person's mental state, leading to all sorts of complications.

Although I spoke of Nordic concepts before, the four mystic planes of existence alluded to in the chant of Squirrel are given Druidic names. The Nordic equivalents of Annwn, Abred, Gwynfid, and Ceugant would be *Utgaror* (or *Jötenheim*), *Midgard*, *Asgaror*, and *Hlioskjálf*.

We interpret them along these lines: Abred stands for this world, this existence, and is the starting place of not only the shamanistic soul journey, but the plane or place where we create our future in the sense that when we reach the age of understanding and accountability for our actions, we are at the crossroads with a path that will, with rebirth, dictate a set of circumstances that we are reborn to. Abred is the place of "Free Will"; in it we have the choice of following the path of good or evil, or even no path at all.

We are reborn in Abred time after time, until the soul has evolved sufficiently to gain the plane or world of Gwynfid, or the place of "Enlightened Souls." This is the place where all the fragments of the Godhead used to seed this world, in the form of individual souls, work in the hope of eventually being reunited and re-absorbed back into the body of God. It is here that all the concepts of the Godhead that we know and call the Old Gods and Goddesses dwell. Here too are to be found the perfected souls, the souls of light and wisdom, who through the centuries have advanced beyond the need of rebirth and who through the wisdom and understanding gained by life after life have finally trodden the spiral path for the last time. Once released from the body, the shamanistic soul may journey to Gwynfid in search of inspiration, wisdom, understanding, and truth.

Annwn (or Annwfn) is the Underworld, the place where the souls of the dead are driven at Candlemas. From here come the "Hounds of Gwyn," red in ear, white in coat, and sharp in fang, invoked as guardians of the circle during its dedication and consecration. It is to Annwn that the soul will go for the period of rest and eventual repurification while awaiting eventual rebirth. Here the Prince of the Underworld sits in judgment upon our actions in this life. When, by an act of free will, we decide to do something or follow a certain course, we now have to answer for the rightness of it. It is here, too, that the innermost soul of a person must absorb the lessons learned in this life and the judgments passed on them, and then hold this in the memory for the period of rest and regeneration until our eventual rebirth. After rebirth and reaching the age of understanding and accountability, we can once again choose to recall or not recall, as the case may be, these past events. If we do choose to recall them, once again we stand at the crossroads with the choice of either learning from our past mistakes and evolving onward and upward, or ignoring them and having to go through the fires of purification and rebirth again.

Likewise, the soul of the Squirrel shaman-priest can enter this world and gain knowledge of how future events and actions will affect both the individual and the group because it is here that the past will be judged and the future then created by that judgment. When that future then becomes the present, we can either accept it and learn by it or ignore and reject it. At some time in this life or the next we will have to pay the price for whatever action we have taken.

Above and beyond these three worlds is Ceugant. Though conceived as a world, sphere, or plane, Ceugant is more a state of being and existence than anything else. Ceugant is the remote timeless and distant place where the first light of inspiration became the energy of creation that first brought order out of chaos, thus creating the universe and all things of the universe. To us, this form of Supreme Godhead is seen as the nameless, formless, age-old and remote Goddess. As old as time itself, as remote as the farthest planet and star of this universe, in Her remoteness, She is above and beyond all things. She is infinity itself, and to try and give form to Her is the same as trying to fix infinity within the framework and boundaries of both time and space. Little wonder that even the most enlightened and spiritually advanced soul can never hope to gain entry to this region, for this is the place of the primordial spirit of creation wherein no earthly conceived and nurtured soul will ever enter. It was from here that the spirit we call creation began, and it is here that the spirit we call creation will finally end.

From the illustration (right), it can be seen that the flow of power or energy is always a downward one from Ceugant to Gwynfid. From Gwynfid to Abred, then Annwn, the power first flows downward, then upward, creating the two-way flow of the spiral pathway. The shamanistic spirit of the Squirrel dancer taps into this force or power-flow pattern as the key to the journey between this world of ours (symbolized by Abred), the Underworld, and the heavens of the "Perfect Souls" who have transcended the need for earthly reincarnation, thus becoming as one with the spirit of the Godhead that manifests itself as the plane of Gwynfid, yet draws the power of its existence from the never-ending flow of energy from the Infinite Being as symbolized by Ceugant.

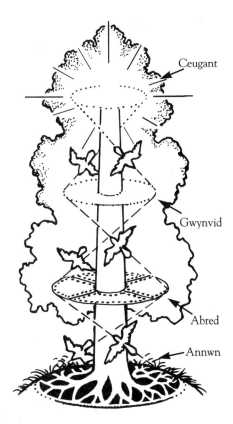

The above diagram is one of the recognized ways of illustrating the concept of the World Tree, Yggdrasill. It can be seen how the power or energy flows downward from Ceugant to Gwynfid, through to Abred and Annwn, then back to Gwynfid, forming a two-way flow both up and down, thus creating the Spiral Path of the Seeking Soul.

Earlier on, I mentioned a group in Oxfordshire who, contrary to normal practice, used the coven stang as part of the workings of the Squirrel rite. Yggdrasill, the World Tree, is traditionally pictured as an ash tree. Likewise, the coven stang is also ash, and where the crossed arrows are mounted on the body of the shaft just over halfway up has a meaning (see illustration, page 106). The stang resembles the World Tree with its base or roots in the Underworld. The crossed arrows represent this world and its symbolic crossroads where we all stand when having to choose which path or way we will follow. The horns represent the world of Gwynfid, the Upper World, where the forms we see as the Godhead dwell along with the souls of those who have

trodden the same spiral path before us. Used in the circle, the coven stang shows all of the key elements that go to make up the mythos of the Squirrel dancer's journey. Once again, I stress that only having seen this once as an invited spectator, I cannot swear to how effective it is. From the little I did see, it seemed to work very well. Indeed, it was one of the most effective keys to the concept that I have ever seen.

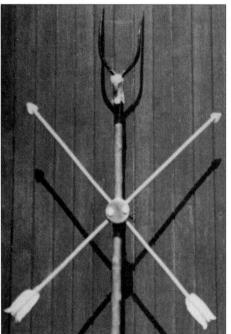

Evan John Jones

This modern Wiccan's stang is a copy of the "Oxfordshire Stang." When planted in the center of the circle and with Squirrel seated on the ground with her back to it, the stang would symbolize the World Tree to the gathering.

The Dance for the Following

In addition to the formal rites of Raven and Squirrel, other members of the masked following may lead the rituals. As I have stressed earlier, all participants are first and foremost coven members and, as such, no different than any other coven member. Taking part in the masked rites means that the people involved have reached a higher stage of development in the art of magical workings and worship. Indeed, one could say that the coven workings serve as a training ground for those who are willing and able to come to terms with the magic of illusion. Even though King Stag, Raven, and Squirrel lead the gathering, each member is a shaman-priest/priestess in their own right. As such, they would expect to play a more active role in the trance play a more active role in the trance workings of the rituals—and rightly so. Through these selfsame trance workings they gain their first insight into what is meant by the term "shamanistic priesthood." To deny them the right to undergo a trance-state contact as a member of the masked gathering would, in a sense, deny the whole principle enshrined in the concept.

Stag, however, continues to set up and consecrate the circle. Following the method employed in the formal rites described earlier, Stag brings everyone into the ritual circle, and they in turn form another circle in the center of it. Stag will then invoke the "Guardians of the Four Quarters," starting in the East and working his way around the circle to finish in the North.

At the East, which is the realm of the Young Horned King, he faces outward, bows, and then, crossing his arms on his chest, he calls on the God, using the words:

Lord of the Eastern skies, the incarnate being symbolized by the morning star, the Young Horned King, born of fire and clothed in raiments of light from the bright morning Sun, armed with a sword that is the first flashing ray of that Sun darting from the Eastern skies to pierce the fading night. We call on You to stand watch on this our sacred place, keeping

us in safety from the forces that are without. In the name of the Goddess, we so do ask.

Stag then moves to the southern quarter where he does the same again and prays:

Our Lady, Goddess of the Night, under whose symbol of the Moon and by its pale light we do acts of worship to Your glory, Yours is the pathway of mystery and hidden things, and like the dark-haired, soft and gentle mother that You are, cradle us in the palm of Your hand and send the shadowy mists of the night to hide us from the forces that are found outside our sacred place. In Your name, so be it done.

Stag goes to the West where, repeating his actions, he then offers up a prayer:

The Dark Lord of the Mound, hooded and cloaked so that none are able to see Your face, we who stand on the threshold of Your domain do humbly pray that You will guide our footsteps through the pathways of Your kingdom to the river that divides this life from the next, and having crossed this river, bring us safely back again to this sacred place that is symbolic of the entrance to

111

Your domain. In the name of
the Goddess, we do so ask.

Stag then goes to the North, and
here again he faces outward and bows;
then with crossed arms, he invokes the
Goddess this aspect:

Pale-Faced Goddess, Mistress
and Queen of the castle
wherein is found the sacred
cauldron of inspiration, we
who have trodden the path
through the realms of the
Underworld to reach Your
sacred halls do call on You
once again to keep shielded
our place of worship from the
forces of chaos that dwell on
the fringes of order and harmony. Guide us, we ask Thee,
to the place of Your cauldron
so that we may partake of the
knowledge that is within.
Then let Your servants tread
safely back along the path to
the place from whence we
came. In all the names by
which You are known, we do
so ask that this be done.

As with the ceremonial rites, the
next thing to be determined is who will
carry the hand staff or wand for the
trance dance. In the ceremonial rite
there were two ways of deciding this;
the same two may be used here. Either
Stag passes the wand around the circle
of dancers, letting the person who feels

the call take it, or he turns his back on
the gathering, and while the wand is
being passed from hand to hand out of
his sight, he offers up a silent prayer to
the Gods along the lines of:

By closing my eyes, I open up
my inner self to the Fates, in
whose laps I have placed the
selection of the leader for this
dance. When they have chosen the one they desire, my
inner being will tell me this.
In the name of the Goddess,
so be it done.

When he feels the time is right,
Stag calls, "Stop!" Whoever has the
staff at this point then becomes the
trance-priest or priestess of the rite.

With this done, the rest of the
group moves outward toward the edge
of the circle, spacing themselves
around it and leaving a cleared area in
the center for the trance priest or
priestess. It will be up to the individual
groups to decide how they will conduct
the ceremony. They can either pace a
deosil Mill while the chosen dancer
stands or sits in the center, letting the
conscious mind empty while at the
same time letting the animistic form of
the mask they are wearing come to the
fore and take over, or they may stand
still while the dancer paces the deosil
Mill, using a long-drawn-out, deep-
pitched, resonant chant of "EEE...

AAA...III...OOO" over and over again, to bring about the body changes and disorientation needed to free the soul in its animistic form to reach out to the world beyond this physical one. The dancer will have to match the pacing of the Mill with the chant. To help them with the rhythm, the rest of the group will either clap their hands or use a drum. While this is going on, Stag will keep himself detached from the ritual, for, depending on how deeply the dancer has gone onto the trance state, he will be the one to ease them down and bring them out.

Having worked this way in the past, I can say from experience that other members of the group besides the designated trance priest/priestess very often do get caught up in the heat of the Mill chant. Indeed, to be effective, the chant and the Mill must he somewhat hypnotic in order to send the dancer into a trance state. At the same time, watching and listening to it can have the same hypnotic effect on the others, so someone has to mentally stand back and be the "observer"—and that someone is Stag.

After a while, the dancer will either flop down on the ground or start to stagger around in an aimless, disoriented manner. At this stage Stag will step in by going to the dancer and either making him or her sit up if they have flopped on the ground or, if they are still on their feet, making them sit down. The dancer needs time to get his or her breath back and for the trance state to fade somewhat before being asked what they have seen or felt.

Remember, unlike the Squirrel rite, these trances are not solely divinatory in nature, so there will be no specific questions to be put or specific answers expected. Instead, these rites are designed to allow the non-office-holding members of the masked gathering to fulfill their function as shamanistic priests of the Old Religion on an individual level as well as a group one. It is through working these rites that the person concerned will find the keys that will trigger, in their mind, the first steps along the individualistic pathway they will have to take to first find, and then come to know, the personalized God or Goddess form or aspect that the mask of Divinity will take on for them and them alone. Thus they learn to meet and to interact with their own guardian God or Goddess spirit form that will stay with them for the rest of their lives—to face an aspect of divinity that with which they will make their priestly pact.

Finally, it would be the duty of Stag to formally close the rite down. This will follow the routine laid out in the rite of Squirrel. Giving the trance dancer time to reach a state of equilibrium, Stag will first fill the cup with wine, holding it aloft while calling on the Goddess to bless it and make it worthy enough to be used as a libation offering. After this, Stag then goes to each quarter in turn and spills a few drops of the wine, starting in the East to the honor of the Young Horned King. Stag then goes to the Southern quarter where a little more wine is spilled to honor the lady in Her guise of the Goddess of the Night. He pours another libation in the West to honor the Dark Lord of the Mound. Finally, Stag goes to the North, where the last of the wine is poured to honor the Pale-Faced Goddess of the North, in Her guise as the Goddess of the Cauldron and the Spinning Castle. With this done, Stag then helps everyone out of the circle and finally pulls up the stakes marking the northern gateway, either throwing them away or taking them with him. If the Following are so inclined, they can hold a small and informal get-together after. This, though not obligatory, serves to help the trance dancer and everyone else involved unwind from a deep and intense magical experience.

Che Dance of Hare

As with all things of a religious or mystical nature, there are always exceptions to the general rule. In the masked rites, this exception is Hare. Whereas all the others follow the same general pattern of working when becoming the trance-state leader of the rite, Hare dancers are a law unto themselves. This happens because Hare is a creature who belongs to the Goddess and Her alone. Because of this traditional relationship between Hare and the Goddess (also discussed in Chapter Three), Hare will respond to their own feelings of what is right or should be done rather than following the accepted way of working. Hare blends three magical traditions: the mystic animal sacred to the Moon Goddess, Diana, the old Druidic tradition of shape-shifting into the form of a hare, and the testimony that hares were among the animal forms that the old witches were reputed to assume when traveling to and from their meetings. Finally, if perhaps not so obviously magical, comes the image of the "Mad March Hare." These animals' wild and careless behavior in the springtime was seen as insanity, and in the past insanity was often blamed on the influences of the Moon, hence the word "lunatic."

Hare's mediumistic madness always has a strange quality about it. In most cases it takes the form of an inspirational and prophetic working, but not in the same way as Squirrel's. Whereas in the rite of Squirrel there is a specific aim to the working as well as a certain amount of control over the proceedings, in the rite of Hare there is none. Hare will do whatever Hare feels like doing, for Hare is the creature of the Goddess and Hers alone to control. In most cases Hare will follow the general trend of the workings, but occasionally will break loose and start doing its own thing.

I remember one occasion when I was present at a working and the wand was settled on Hare. Everyone moved to their positions on the edge of the circle. Hare started to do the deosil Mill, then suddenly left the circle and wandered off a short way. We, knowing the tradition of the Hare dancer, stayed where we were, letting Hare go off on his own. Getting some distance from the circle, Hare started to do a solitary Mill for a while and then, all of a sudden, sank down on his knees as though kneeling in homage to some invisible figure. After a while, Hare returned to the circle, looking rather dazed but definitely not in the usual trance state that we had expected. Seeing this, Stag decided that it was now time to wind the rite down. After this was done and Hare questioned, all he had to say was that he had seen the Goddess in Her aspect of the dark-haired mother, and for a moment, She had smiled on him. For the first time Hare had found his Goddess.

This experience with Hare sums up rather neatly what the whole of the masked rites are about. Just as Hare is unpredictable, so are all the trance workings. From the moment a person steps into the circle to the moment when the dancer comes out of the trance, no one can say for sure just what is going to happen. Unlike the coven workings where things tend to follow a predictable line—apart from Raven and Squirrel, both of whom follow a precise way of working—what happens is in the hands of the Gods. What shape or form they take on while in contact with the trance dancer will always be a highly individual one. Once a person has seen the Godhead in a specific form, this is the aspect they will see each time. Each individual has to open themselves up to the Gods or the Goddess while in first-state trance. In return, they receive a trance-state vision of the Godhead in a shape or form that is solely for them, and no other. I suppose one could claim that if this vision appears in association with, for instance, the Boar or the Cat-masked dancer, they would then become the Cat or Boar priest or priestess to the Gods. The masked rites are a gathering of individual priests and priestesses who work together the divinatory rites of the magic of illusion. The mask creates the illusion within the circle while the spirit slips into an animistic form and is then free to find the reality of the Goddess in one of Her many and varied forms.

Whatever mask you wear, you should offer up a short prayer before beginning the rite. Here is one that I have heard used and have used myself in the past. Where I have used the word "Cat," you may substitute the name of the bird or animal mask you are wearing.

> I am brother/sister to the Cat
> and call on the spirit of Cat to
> descend upon me once again
> in its mystic form, so that I
> and the others of this gather-
> ing may come to know more
> fully the nature of the call
> that has brought us to this
> place of worship. In the name
> of the Goddess, so be it done.

Choughts on Crance and Recovery

Throughout this book, whenever trance has been mentioned, I have emphasized bringing the trance subject back safely to this world. Make no mistake, trance is a dangerous thing to dabble in, even though it is a recognizable magical tool of long standing and usage. Neverthe-less, in the hands of people who are accustomed to working in this way, there is little or no risk involved with the trance form. One thing that should be stressed most forcibly at this point is that first-state trance must be self-induced. I have, in the past, known about groups who, for some reason best known to themselves, have experi-mented with both drugs and hypnosis to try to gain something akin to trance state. In my eyes, this is a lethal combi-nation that puts the subject into great danger, both physically and mentally. It has no place within the masked rites, nor is it a short-cut to the opening of both mind and spirit that comes through working the shamanistic ritu-als. Because the trance is self-induced, any help that the person involved in the trance working gets from the rest of the group is limited, in effect, to their help in creating the right atmosphere for the working to take effect.

The actual changes to the body that take place during the working fol-low a distinct pattern. In the first instance, there is the feeling that everything going on around you settles into a distinct pattern or rhythm that corresponds to the pacing of the Mill. As the trance deepens, you feel that you know what is going on, yet at the same time you feel somewhat divorced from it, as though you are doing the motions on another level, while look-ing down at your body going through the same motions. A little later, there is the blackness, only broken by the floating circles of light that seem to fill your vision. Gradually these are replaced by repeated zig-zag patterns flashing across your vision while

116

changing color. With each change, the colors get brighter and stronger. In the final stages, within the center of this pulsating zig-zag effect, you start seeing vertical and horizontal bands of white light coming together to form a grid. In my case, in the next moment I was an owl.

As hard as it is to explain, I will try to write down just how it felt. The whole experience seemed to work on two levels. On one level, I knew who I was and that I had still retained my body shape, yet at the same time there was an outer skin or shape in the form of an owl surrounding me. So vivid was this impression that not only could I see with the eyes of an owl, I also knew what it felt like to look out of those selfsame eyes because there were two distinct and separate *mes*. There was me as I knew myself to be, and there was the owl-me who could not only see and feel the feathers on my body but could move them as well.

Perhaps the strangest thing of all was that whatever the owl-me was doing, the other me that was inside the owl body responded with the same feelings and actions. It was like being two distinct and separate entities intertwining with each other and having to act as one, yet at the same time remaining two separate identities. Then suddenly I found myself being propped up by one of the members while Stag was talking

quietly to me and encouraging me to return to this world.

It must have taken a good five or ten minutes for me to summon up enough energy to join the others for the closing of the rite, and then to walk away from the site. For quite a few hours afterwards, I felt as though I was still two people within the same body. With the passing of time, this gradually faded, leaving only the vivid memory of what had occurred. One thing I should make clear is that I did not tap into some marvelous vein of prophecy, nor did I experience any startling revelations. The effects or changes that occurred were far more subtle and far-reaching than that. It took much longer than one would expect for the changes to be realized. So what was the point of it all? In my case, when something is bothering me and I don't know the answer or how to deal with it, I sit down and relax for a while, letting my mind go empty, and sure enough, I start to feel the presence of owl creeping over me and fitting me like a second skin. Though the feeling is not as vivid as my first experience, I still get the feeling of the "owl-me" blending in with the other me. From somewhere, the answers that I have been searching for appear, and instinctively I know that they will be the right ones. When I say that the spirit of the owl is still with me and still part of me while at the same time responding to some of my needs, I mean just that.

An equally important experience is to actually see a person in first-state trance. Watching how they behave while in a trance and learning how to help them out of it is part of that. When the dancer first starts the deosil Mill, there will no noticeable change at first. Gradually you will notice the pacing of the Mill becoming more and more mechanical, while starting to match the clapping of the hands or the beat of the drum. After a while, you get the distinct impression that the dancer's stride is getting longer and longer, while at the same time he or she totally ignores what is underfoot. I remember on one occasion when the dancer kept treading on the same large tuft of grass each time they went around. Not only did it look painful, it was—the person concerned actually sprained an ankle treading on the turf, yet was totally oblivious to the pain caused by this sprain. In this instance it was not just a case of grinning and bearing it for a couple of circuits of the circle. This particular Mill went on for another twenty minutes or so, and from what we could see of the person's face, we could tell they were no longer in this world. In the end, there was a sudden and total collapse. Stag and a couple of us then went to the dancer, getting them to sit up. Stag talked to them gently while one of us

massaged the back of their neck, and the trance gradually faded.

The final step to the recovery was to get them on their feet and walking. At first, this was a case of holding them up and talking to them, calling them by name. As they recovered, the faraway expression slowly faded from the face and they were once again able to move freely on their own. Finally Stag closed the circle down in the usual way (described earlier in this book).

Even people who do not fully enter trance will benefit from the informal get-together after the rite. By the sheer nature of the working, emotions will be heightened among the members, especially in the case of the trance subject. In addition, as with any serious working of this nature, anagogic memories arise in the working of the rite—symbolic insights that are hard to verbalize immediately and that should not necessarily be taken literally. The informal gathering after the ritual is the ideal place to talk over what has actually happened, as opposed to what people think occurred.

Many people, when attending this sort of meeting, fall under the spell of this false memory, which in part is brought about by heightened emotions. It is dangerous to carry these over into normal life outside the circle and the gathering; doing so can lead to all sorts of complications. People have started to imagine that the small, everyday accidents that occur are brought about because someone or something "has it in for them." Just precisely what or who, as well as why, is one of those things that no one has quite been able to put their finger on, but occur it does and far more often than people think. (I am reminded of how young medical students often become convinced that they are suffering or have the symptoms of every disease they read about in their textbooks.) Laughing and joking is perhaps one of the best ways I know of to "earth" a ritual and bring things back to normal. Every Witch has to learn, and learn fast, to separate the occult or magical life from the life of the world we live in and to keep them separate. In the case of these workings, because we are dealing with trance state and illusion in both a magical and a mental sense, failure to do so means that illusion will spill over into this world, along with the seeds of madness and eventual self-destruction, the worst trap a magician can fall into. Bringing the magical rite back to earth and grounding it has always been regarded as an inherent part of the ritual, just as important a part of the working of the rite as the trance itself. Other groups earth their rituals in other ways, which to them work satisfactorily. They must decide for themselves how they will deal with the after-effects of the magical working, and once finding what suits them best, stick with it, as well as try to gain some insight into why a particular method works best for them.

A Group Purification Ritual

One last suggestion: I personally prefer that a magical working group undergo some sort of yearly purification ritual. To be fair about it, this is something I *like* to see done, rather than claiming it to be a vital part of the old tradition and something that should always be done. I suppose it could be looked at in the same light as the old Roman custom of every February ritually cleansing the house of all the influences and spirits of the past year, leaving it clean for the coming year. Any purification rite will be done in a coven setting rather than by the masked dancers.

Even though this book deals mainly with the masked rites, I always stress that the masked rites themselves are considered as part of the overall coven workings, done by the more experienced members of the group.

Even though the Lady might be one of the dancers concerned, she would be the priestess of the purification rite and would do it in the name of the coven rather than the masked gathering.

119

The elaborateness of this purification would be up to the group concerned. As an example, I include a modified version of our own coven rite for this occasion. Because this is a personal rather than a formal ceremony, there is no fixed date for it to be done. For myself, I prefer some time in February after Candlemas, but any group doing this would decide on their own date rather than be bound by anyone else.

Because water will be sprinkled around, the purification rite is usually held outdoors, but if people don't mind water being splashed around inside a room, then by all means hold it indoors if this is preferred. As this is a ritual purification rather than a ceremonial one, the circle itself will be a fully charged and consecrated one, and inside it will be the usual bowl, bottle of water, and a small bundle of twigs bound together to form a brush. Because water is involved, it will be the Lord of the West rather than East who will assist the Lady in its consecration.

With everyone gathered inside the circle and the Lady having closed it in the usual way, instead of taking her usual place in the North, she stays by the fire or, if indoors, the candle lantern. As the coven is not asking inspiration and knowledge from this working, only a cleansing, the Lady would open the rite with a prayer along the lines of this:

I pray that the old Gods and Guardians of this our gathering see and understand our need to be cleansed from our past and in this understanding lift from us the effects of the things done by us in the past year. Whereas once in the past a blood price would have been paid for this absolving, we now offer water, without which none may live in its stead, thus being a symbol of forgetfulness and oblivion that is to be found in the timeless river, using it to wash away our past, making us clean once again and fit to follow our chosen way of working. In our Lady's name, so be it done.

Pausing for a few moments before calling West to her, she then asks him to join her in the center of the circle. West will then hand her the bottle of water before picking up the bowl for the Lady to pour it in. This she does and then says:

By the powers granted to me as a priestess of the Goddess, I charge this water with the powers invoked for the washing clean of souls.

She then puts the bottle down, and taking the bowl from West, raises it on high as she would the cup during the knife, raises it and then lowers the point into the water, while at the same time saying:

> Thus, with the act of joining knife to water symbolizing the joining of the Goddess with the Young Horned King, so the water in this vessel shall be charged with the powers of the sacred blood of sacrifice to pay for the removal of that which is upon us. In our Lady's name, so be it done.

He then kisses the Lady. Sheathing his knife, he takes the bowl from her. The Lady then takes the twig brush and dips it in the water. Flicking a few drops first on herself and then on West, she proceeds to do the same to the rest of the congregation, using the words:

> Thus with this illustration given in the knowledge of the rightness of the act, I wash away from us all the things of the past. In this token wash-ing is the knowledge that all that has gone on before has now been taken from us, leav-ing us clean as the newly washed babe. Thus clean in both spirit and body, we are ready once again to work the mysteries of our faith. In our Lady's name, so be it done.

There is a silence of a minute or so before the Lady says:

> As for the charged water that is left, from the earth it came, to the earth I return it. In the name of the Goddess, so be it done.

The rite is now effectively over, but should the group feel they would like to include a token deosil ring dance as part of the ceremony, by all means do so. However, remembering the nature of the rite, there would be no gathering for a feast afterwards; the leaving of the circle effectively marks the closing of the rite.

Notes

1. While salt is a traditional symbol of magical purity, some persons may object to spreading it directly on the ground, because in large quantities it sterilizes the soil. Those persons may wish to substitute chalk, grain, or pollen.

2. Brian Branston, *Gods of the North* (London: Thames and Hudson, 1980), 76.

3. Branston, 34.

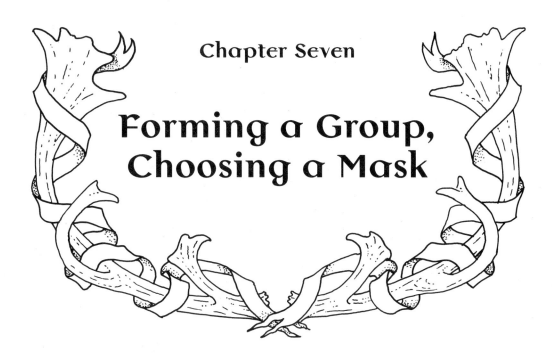

Chapter Seven

Forming a Group, Choosing a Mask

By now, you may have some questions. The first might be this: the masked rites are all well and good for the larger, formal coven or gathering, but can a smaller group work with the same concept?

Other questions might be: What form should masks take? Are they full-facial masks or what? How does someone settle on what mask to wear? Do the masks change depending on where in the world you live?

Some readers might find it strange that this chapter has been included so late in the book, instead of at the beginning. My reason is that the full concept and aims of the masked rites can only be looked at in the context of a full working group of thirteen. By contrast, to start off with the concept from the point of view of a small group wanting to work them, and then to expand the concept as the numbers of the group increased would make what is already a complicated subject even more complex. Not only that, by linking the number of members to certain stages of advancement within the concept means that instead of leaving the group free to choose their own way of working their own rites, you would in fact be tying their hands by saying that with N number of members, you will have only reached such and such a stage, and can only work in such and such a way. By being well versed in the fundamental basics of both the technique of masked rites and the concept itself, both can be examined in depth with more information being added. At the same time, the practical workings may develop at a speed to suit the group and the types of persons involved.

However, this does not preclude a smaller group from involvement. Suppose that a few friends are working together and feel drawn to the idea of the masked rituals, but they are too few to form a reasonably sized group or a full gathering of thirteen. Then the answer is to carry over the concept of the mask into their normal workings.

For example, instead of using Craft names in circle as most covens do, each person takes on the name of one of the masks, if they are so willing. Not all members are, and the important thing is that each person must feel drawn to the mask they choose. In this way, they become known by the name of the mask—to the rest of the group, they become Brother/Sister Cat, Hare, Boar, or whatever. This will generate a feeling that there is something special abut the mask and the person wearing it. The sensation that something different is being worked within a coven or group will affect everyone in it.

As more members join, the conditions laid down for the new coven members to become dancers alter too. Ideally, no one would be introduced to

the masked workings until they had served their initiation period. Then and only then would they be allowed to witness the masked dancers working.

If by then the group has expanded to more than thirteen people, full members would be introduced gradually into the workings, at first serving as an understudy to one of the dancers and learning the techniques from them. When finally conversant with the working of the rites, members may take turns wearing a particular mask for the rituals, thus giving everyone who is willing the opportunity to follow the path of the shamanistic Witch-priest or priestess. The only office that would not be divided between members is the office of the Stag. Stag is Stag and the master of the rites until they feel the need to stand down for good. Then a new Stag is picked from the ranks of the others—usually the next-longest-serving member of the dancers.

Remember, unlike the initiate to the coven, the masked dancer is a Witch, in the full sense of the word, who has decided to advance along the path of the shamanistic priest or priestess of the trance workings by studying the concepts and techniques involved in trance workings and getting the feel of them in theory first. No matter how small the group is, it can make a start along a path that should eventually lead to a full gathering of thirteen dancers.

In the case of two, three, or more people, just as in the case of the newly started full group of thirteen, each person will have to first discover the aspect or mask best suited to their personality and work from there. When, and only when, each individual feels fully at home with the idea and wearing of the mask in a physical sense—and more importantly in a mental sense—will the whole aim of the masked rite start to fall into place. Once again, I would stress that the masked rites are nothing more than a theatrical drama/ritual that creates an illusion which in the end becomes reality within the circle. By entering into the spirit of the rites, a person is allowing the spirit enshrined in the mask to enter them for the duration of the rite.

When a person has expressed a desire to adopt a certain mask, by taking time and slowly working up to the introduction to the full ritual and concept, they can get the feel of the mask as a personal identity. They can learn to relate to the mask in such a way that when the time comes for them to take their place in the full rites, they will possess full knowledge and understanding of what lies behind it. Far better to slowly introduce the person to the dance than to let them come in cold and find their own way.

Robin Larsen

Here a group of mask-makers from the Rainbow Community model their creations.

125

Additionally, this slow introduction to the rites will also give the person concerned a chance to find out if he or she is suited to one particular mask rather than another, The idea of someone coming along and saying, "You will be Hare or what-have-you" and allocating the masks in this arbitrary way defeats the whole aim of the concept. Taking up a mask must be an act of free will. When each person wanting to take part is given the opportunity to find the mask and aspect they feel most in sympathy with, when they finally take their place in the trance rite circle, they will then truly be able to claim the mantle of the shamanistic witch-priest/priestess and the servant of that particular manifestation of the Godhead.

When a person tries working with one mask, decides that it is not for them, and then wants to go on to try another, let them, for this is the only way that they will find what they truly want and are suited for. Every one of us must first find our place within the rites and then learn to grow into the part we have decided to follow.

As the masked rites evolved, we developed a ceremonial side. Unlike cultures such as the Bushmen's that have never lost the technique of using trance as part of their esoteric tradition, we have. Though the ceremonial rites are an act of worship in themselves, they should also be a training ground for the full magical workings that will come later. During the ceremonial workings, even though there is no serious magical intent, the group still has to create both the inward and outward conditions by saying, "I am brother-sister to the hare," or whatever is being represented by the mask worn. The person saying this must really feel that kinship and really mean what they say.

In many ways this is the hardest part of working the masked rites, because for so long we have turned our backs on this method of working. Unlike our ancestors, who were accustomed to seeing this sort of magical rite as well as understanding what lay behind it, we are not. A surprising number of people, who for the first time take part in a masked rite, are somewhat self-conscious about it. In most cases people get the feeling that it is all rather "theatrical," which of course it is. We create an illusion that in the end, becomes reality. The mask is nothing more than an outward expression of the magical illusion, while the inner self or soul shape-shifts into the character that the mask portrays, thereby becoming the aimed-for reality within the illusion.

Many things have to be taken into consideration before deciding on the form the masks will take. Much comes down to cost, availability, or as in the case of most groups, having in the group someone with enough skills to make the masks out of papier-mâché or other materials.

Another factor in mask-making is the location chosen for the rites. Originally, rites such as these were part of the religious observances of the population. Participants could work undisturbed. I suspect that many of us have a secret outdoor working place that we have found but do not actually have permission to use. In most cases, no one actually notices what is going on because it does not create a problem for others, but in the case of the masked rites, because of the formal and elaborate setting in which they are normally held, the chances of the group being noticed and therefore investigated is that much greater.

Groups that can work in total privacy, such as the Oxfordshire group that I mentioned earlier, are more fortunate. The Oxfordshire group, for instance, has access to a large barn that they can use for indoor workings. When working indoors, they would use the very formal version of the rites with full facial masks for the Following, including Mare, and with a horned helmet and mask for Stag. When working outdoors in a less formal atmosphere, instead of using complete masks, they wear a "token mask" in the form of an animal or bird-head badge (notice the badges in Chapter 3 accompanying dis-

cussions of each of the thirteen animals). Strangely enough, the idea of the token mask badge came from the initial stage in their working of the masked rites; they formalized the concept by introducing full facial masks at a much later date.

This may seem to be just the reverse of what you would expect—that it would be the more-experienced groups who would work without masks, time and practice having made them more familiar and at home with the concept. But no, in most cases it is the other way round. It comes back to the old, old concept of presenting one face to the world for all to see, while behind that face is another one that is turned toward the Godhead, and this is the face that only the Godhead will see. In one way, it is just like rubbing your hand down over your face to remove the make-up or mask that is the usual face you present to the world at the start of the rite. By drawing your hand down over your face, you are symbolically exposing the mentally created animistic face or mask of the shaman/priest or priestess of the rites. Not the easiest thing to do I agree, but there again, the path of the shamanistic witch-priest or priestess has never been an easy one to tread.

There is one advantage in wearing the token badge rather than starting off wearing the full mask. It gives everyone a chance to come to the concept slowly, while at the same time determining if they are suited to this type of working. Make no mistake, there are those who, no matter how hard they try, will never be able to come to terms with the masked rites. To push these people toward the masked rites when they are obviously unsuited to them is not only damaging to the person concerned, but it also tends to disrupt the feel and flow of the rites as well. It is far better to let those who are reluctant remain in the coven where they rightfully belong than to try and push them along the path further than they wish or feel they should go.

Once again, it has to be stressed that the masked rites are not something that replaces the coven or group workings, even though it may be assumed from what has been written that the masked rites are a higher grade of working so therefore the masked gathering have a higher grade within the group. Just as the coven is nothing more than a gathering of individuals who have come together to worship and work in a certain way, the same can be said for the masked gathering who have come together to work in a different way from the normal group activities, yet still remaining within the framework of the group structure. When the dancers work their shamanistic divinatory trance state rites, they

do so in the name of the group and for the benefit of the group, because all knowledge and understanding gained through them become the common property of the group or coven, to be shared by all.

The Masked-Rite Calendar

Within the calendar of the ritual year, there are four dates that are immediately excluded from our performance of the masked rites. These are the "great sabbats" of the coven: Candlemas (February 2), May Eve (April 30), Lammas (August 1), Halloween (October 31). Everyone should be present for these religious celebrations. Also ruled out are the monthly esbats, even though less formal and more "come if you can, or work with your partner or on your own" times that are still firm and fixed dates for ritual acts of worship, simple ones though they may be. They should be looked upon as a joining together of kindred souls in a shared communion and worship of the Old Gods and the Goddess, or in the case of the solitary person, a solitary act of worship and communion—the times where very often the Goddess will take part of your soul and make it Hers forever.

If the group has an indoor place for working, then there is no problem with performing the masked rites. If the group is forced to work outside, then the best time would be as near as possible to the full of the Moon, during the warmer months of the year. After all, no one in their right mind wants to be out on a hillside on a pitch-black and ice-cold night working a long ritual that includes some of the people standing around for the duration of the rite. Far better to plan on working from the end of May through the end of September. The reason for working at the Full Moon is that it gives a better level of light as well as helps to create the right atmosphere for a successful working. Those who have never had the pleasure of working out on a warm, balmy moonlit night have missed one of the pleasures and magical moments that the Craft has to offer. Stand on a hill looking out across a silent countryside bathed in the pale and silvery light of the Moon with every shadow cast by the trees seemingly haunted by the shades of the past, and the very air itself seems charged with a special sort of magic. You also know that the Goddess herself is very close, and her presence can be felt all around you.

I always advise against overdoing the masked rites as well. Personally, I have always held that the masked gathering should never meet more than two or three times a year. Four would be the maximum I'd recommend; anything over this number would drain the dancers of all psychic energy and eventually make the meetings feel flat and empty.

There are countless reasons why the number of trance workings should be strictly limited, but for the sake of brevity, only the basic ones will be discussed. In the first place, everyone has only a limited amount of psychic energy to draw on, and like a battery, too much use will drain it dry. Each magical working drains a certain amount of this energy or magical power away from the person. As the dancers are involved in the coven magical workings as well as the trance workings, the latter impose an even greater drain on their limited supply of psychic power. To recharge the psychic batteries once again a person must just simply leave as long a time as they can between each magical working.

Another point to bear in mind is that in the coven rites, at both the sabbats and the esbats, a distinction is made between coven magical workings and coven celebration workings. The celebratory acts of worship, instead of draining energy, should attract to each person a measure of the peace and understanding that comes from the worship and presence of the Goddess. Since the masked rites are not celebratory in the same way, they could in no way replace any of the energy used in doing them. This is yet another reason why the masked rites must always be seen as complementary to the coven workings and not as something outside the coven framework and coven concept.

Consider also the mental impact that the masked workings can have on a person. This is something that has to be considered with any form of occultism, and in the case of the trance workings, a lot more thought than usual has to be given to such things. The masked rites can only be for the strong-willed and most level-headed members of any group. Someone who is not so stable and level-headed or not so experienced may be pushed by working the masked rites toward fits of depression and an eventual nervous breakdown. Through contact and using the powers so raised, certain people gradually develop the feeling that they are the masters of the power instead of its servants and try to manipulate the power to a different end than is intended. Any form of circle magic involves potentially dangerous but neutral power that, in the case of constant abuse, can and eventually will rebound on the practitioner.

Knowing that the power is there waiting to be tapped, used, and manipulated by a group very often leads to the assumption that because past results have been rewarding, the leading members of the group have some sort of divine right to use this in any way they see fit. Not so! Even though on the surface they appear to be masters of the power, they are in fact still the servants of it. Eventually, abuse of the circle power will lead to self-delusion and eventual self-destruction. Unlike the coven workings where this form of abuse tends to act on one individual, in the masked working, because of the interdependency of the group upon each other, it tends to involve the whole gathering. Where one person has sown the first seeds of self-destruction, in time the whole group will be dragged into it, starting with the weaker and less stable members. Like the ripples from a stone thrown into a pond, the effects will spread to overwhelm the others.

"The pitcher that goes to the well the most is the first to be broken," hence all trance-state workings must be treated with caution as a sparingly used way of reaching out to find the Godhead. Exercising restraint in working these rites is one of the very basic lessons the Faith should teach us. Combine restraint with knowledge and wisdom—knowledge of how to create the conditions for the generating of magical power and the tapping in and manipulating of the forces thus raised, plus the wisdom to know the effects it can have on people, as well as knowing when and how often they should be invoked.

Finally, remember that in the past, trance and trance workings were once looked upon as normal working tools of the Old Religion. With the coming of Christianity and the conversion of the ruling classes to that faith, even though in many cases it was a purely nominal one, the more formal aspects of Pagan religions were disrupted, eventually driven underground, and finally fragmented. Much of the old knowledge of the trance workings became lost. Because they were formal and therefore more organized in a ritual way, they were extremely difficult to keep hidden from preying eyes in the same way as the coven rites were. Little wonder that, in the end, they were abandoned as a working tool and much later more or less forgotten or half-remembered as something the "Old Ones" used to do way back in the past.

In addition, the Old Faith underwent radical change in outlook, direction, and symbolism during medieval times. During this time period the seal was set on the recognizable form that Witchcraft would take in the future, one that is with us today. Strangely, it was the orthodox church with its near-monopoly on learning that created the climate for changes in many of the aspects of the faith. In the age of what could be described as the "New

This cave painting at Cogul, from the Palaeolithic period, shows women dancing.

131

Learning," many native traditions of the old Anglo-Saxon faith were overwhelmed with the influx of both Arabian and Jewish esoteric writings, and these in turn were firmly rooted in both classical Greek and Roman Pagan traditions. The faith not only adapted to these changes but also was able to take the symbolism involved and turn it into a form of Witchcraft that today is recognizably English.

For example, Diana, Hecate, the Pan-like figure of the Horned God, and many other divine aspects owe more to the Classical Pagan world than a purely Saxon one. In one medieval witchcraft illustration, you see portrayed the use of the sieve and shears for divination. This owes more to a Greek than a Saxon source, as well as being known by the Greek name of *conscinomancy*, an ancient and complicated method of divination. Astrology, alchemy, necromancy, and the calling up of devils or the spirits of the dead were all more or less introduced into the occult world as part of the blossoming of medieval culture and learning. Looking at the picture of witchcraft prior to the witch trials and persecutions, you would see a remarkable blending together of Germanic, Celtic, and Classical Mediterranean lore and magical practices, which later on would absorb both Jewish and Arabian occult sciences.

Most certainly any grand master of a gathering would have belonged to the educated, literate classes and therefore would have not only been able to get his hands on this occult "New Learning" material, but would have been interested enough to study it as well. Little wonder that many long-held native practices and traditions would simply fade away and eventually be forgotten. Because of the grand master's high status in the eyes of the congregation, as new concepts and perceived images spread downward and outward from the top, anything he said would have been more or less a divine pronouncement from the living representative of the Incarnate God on earth.

As more and more occult works were translated from Latin into the vernacular, this knowledge became more widespread. To the Church, the most worrisome thing about all this was the way that the New Learning or knowledge penetrated the very fabric of the Church itself. It is not surprising to find that many of the clergy were brought to trial under the Witchcraft Acts, nor is it surprising that the Church acted against witches and magic when in 1317 C.E., the Bishop of Cahors was tried and executed for attempts on the life of Pope John XXII, in league with an unnamed Jewish magician and other elusive figures. One charge concerned the alleged smuggling into the Papal Court of certain unspecified magical images and inscriptions. Another telling point that can be drawn from these trials is that even though high-ranking persons were involved, it was usually common people from either towns or villages who actually performed the magical workings. Magic at a rural community level might to a certain degree have passed unnoticed or at least been tacitly accepted, but when it reached into the Curia itself, some form of drastic action had to be taken.

Under the twin blows of first the influx of new and therefore strange occult learning appealing to the educated classes because of its classical content, and later the witch persecutions, the old Anglo-Saxon Witchcraft became a casualty, being greatly changed by all this. In some ways it is a bit like the "trendy set" who buy a certain make of foreign car because it is "in" and totally ignore the home-produced car. No matter that the home-produced model gives better value for the money and so on, the one thing held against it is that it is not foreign and it is not a status symbol. Likewise with occult learning: the home-grown stuff couldn't be all that good because the common people worked it. Anyhow, no one wrote learned tomes on it, forbidden though they would have been. It was precisely this attitude that destroyed

the continuity of the old Saxon faith which lay at the roots of English Witchcraft and replaced much of it with the semi-Classical images and symbols of the modern Witch tradition.

What did remain of the old Saxon images and mythos would with time become equated with its classical counterparts, and the two would then gradually blend, forming the images and mythos that we know and recognize as the Witch tradition of today. Even though the Craft may have changed its outlook and direction, at the same time the whole concept of witchcraft, even though fragmented and suppressed, must have revitalized itself while drawing a certain amount of strength from blending. The evidence for all this? Unlike the Saxon mythos, which in general was never written down, the new occult learning as well as the new witch tradition and learning, was first circulated in an underground and

This very old horned mask is called the New Dorset Ooser. It is one of the last known shamanic masks that have been found in England. It is described in Margaret A. Murray's *God of the Witches*.

covert way maybe, but circulated it was and is. Today, being a Witch is no longer a criminal offense, and to own a book on witchcraft is no longer an excuse for a burning.

One positive effect of the change to a more classical form of symbolism was to make the old concepts more universal. Looking at the evidence of the continental witch trials, even though some of the coven figures may have been known by different names, their status and functions within the coven would have been recognized by any English witch of the relevant time.

So why try to turn the clock back by introducing the masked rites, which to some might seem a retrograde step? For one thing, we are not looking at a specific Anglo-Saxon concept as such. The theory and practice of trance-state workings stem from ancient magical tradition, once part of the development of a religious awareness in humankind. Through the use of trance and trance-state workings early people tried to bridge the gap between their world and the spirit world, with the intent of enlisting the magic of the spirit world to help them survive. In doing this, they realized that there was more to life than just survival, which in turn led to imposing on the basic group or tribe certain dos and don'ts in the form of tribal taboos. Eventually this led to the laying down of the moral and

ethical codes of conduct that are the basic premise of any religion, designed to regulate the conduct between humans and Deity as well as between humans themselves. As humankind advanced and the idea of a more formalized and corporate form of worship to the Gods evolved, more and more the old ways were neglected. Thus, in many cultures, the concept of the trance workings became lost—in others, it hung on while developing in many different ways.

In the case of Anglo-Saxon trance magic, it too was replaced by another form of Witch tradition. This present tradition is now in a state of flux with new ideas and interpretations coming to the fore. Perhaps this is as good a time as any to take the concept out of the closet of history, dust it off, and reexamine it to see what it has to offer us today.

There is no way that the original Anglo-Saxon and Nordic trance concepts, techniques, and traditions could ever be recovered, nor should they be even if it were possible. Conditions change, times change, and what we would now expect to gain from the trance workings would not necessarily be the same as what was sought and gained in the past. Instead, let us take the old concept and reshape it to suit the needs and aspirations of today's group or coven. Trance is a magical tool, and the ability to use trance is not only common to all but is also part of our physical make-up. Therefore, not to take this ability, sharpen it up, and develop it, means that in a sense we are turning our backs on a God-given faculty. Not to use it also means that the coven or group is not expanding its frontiers of knowledge and understanding in the way it should, but rather standing still on the path of spiritual development.

When the two types of working—the masked rites and the normal coven sabbats and esbats—are both performed, things brought back from the trance workings can change the direction that the full coven is taking, much in the same way as a spontaneous happening during a rite can change it from a formal rite into an inspirational working—the sort of working where the Goddess takes the group by the hands and starts them off on another path of inspiration and worship. Many things can come from the trance rites that sooner or later will be of use to the coven as well as to the individual. New light thrown on certain ways of working, new ideas to advance and broaden the old concepts, new paths of knowledge and understanding to be explored—all of these can come from the trance-rite workings. As they do, these new ways will be for that coven, and that coven only.

Hindu mythology speaks of the god Indra's net, where each jewel must reflect all the others—so the trance state workings must reflect the coven workings and vice-versa. Only then will both concepts come together to create a whole and well-rounded working tradition, one that will in time enhance the perceived view and image people have of the Craft and what can be gained from being a member.

Adapting the Masked Rites to Your Location

The Masked Rites of Tubal Cain were developed in Britain, and the masks of the Following reflect the historic fauna of the British Isles. A very strong argument can be made, however, that it would be a mistake simply to transfer them intact to other regions of the globe. True, our distant Pagan ancestors may not have devoted much time to the question of cultural inheritance versus being rooted to the lands to which they migrated. The sagas speak of a Norseman invoking Thor on the shores of North America (this during the time when Iceland and Greenland were largely becoming Christian). Likewise, we have the enigmatic and inexplicable carved ogham inscriptions of North America, seemingly written in a Celtic tongue, that appear to mention Celtic deities.[1]

135

A thousand years later, however, the issues are different. The modern Pagan movement in all its forms has grown and spread in lands such as North America and Australia with their bloody histories of deliberate cultural eradication. Even in Canada, where the European-Native conflicts were not always as warlike as in the United States, the end results in terms of cultural and religious hegemony were much the same. Undoubtedly, a major reason for the spread of modern Witchcraft into these lands has been that it offers a form of "earth religion" that does not appear to intrude on the rites of aboriginal peoples. Modern Witches, for the most part, take pains not to appropriate the rites and practices of these peoples except in the most general ways—for example, using sagebrush or native resins such as copal in ritual. As Pagans, we do not assert that a new land was given to us by God the Father to transform as we see fit.

While this attitude is based on respect for other people's traditions, it contains one hidden hazard. By blindly revering the lands and practices of our spiritual or ancestral origins, we may neglect to make connections *where we are*. In the words of one Native American writer, Carol Lee Sanchez, who has sought to bridge this gap: "The next step is for non-Tribal Americans to acknowledge their own connections to *this* land (through birth or adoption) and to revere this land more than they revere and abstract [the] notion of freedom symbolized by their Declaration of Independence, their Constitution, and the flag that flew over their conquest and disenfranchisement of approximately forty million native peoples."[2] Of course, Sanchez's basic idea would apply outside the United States as well. If an Australian, for example, merely copied the forms of British Witchcraft without considering how to connect them to Australia's unique environment, would this not lead to a new form of spiritual separation? Only a land-based mythos, a deep spiritual connection not just "to the Earth" in general, but to ecological systems and bioregions will reverse centuries of environmental rape and plunder.

When assuming the masks, as with working with shamanic power animals, consider local realities. Mare is virtually universal, thanks to humanity's love of horses, but Stag is not—in North America, the bull elk is a related species to the British red deer stag. Boar is in North America by adoption too: effectively wild populations are found in parts of northern California, the Arizona desert, and the southern Appalachians. Raven, for instance, is the same in North America as Europe. In addition to sensing what mask attracts you, consider working with your own power animals to determine what masks you might wear.[3]

Some Pagan writers have gone so far as to suggest that working with non-native animal energies may be harmful. "I never call energies from another ground onto a place unless those energies are ones that have business in that place," said an Australian writer, Spider Redgold. "For instance, if you have read a book about Celtic magic with the energy of Fox or Badger, it is not appropriate to call Fox and Badger energy into the Australian bush. It is very upsetting to the local spirits." Once she was present when someone reading a book about North American sweat lodges called bear and wolf spirits "into the ground where the largest predator was the dingo." Two years later, the dreamkeepers of the place were still upset.[4]

What is needed is a middle way, then, between following a system that might not be right for where you are, and taking a "look but don't touch" approach that makes the task of being rooted seem insurmountable. It is not an "either/or" situation but a "both/and" one. Witches can be blenders and weavers of the old and the new, the exotic and the domestic, as long as they do so with respect and knowledge. Someone wishing to work the masked rites outside their region of origin might wish, therefore, to consider the animals that are native to that other region. What traditional stories exist about them? What similarities and dissimilarities turn up, for instance, between Raven in Celtic and Germanic lore and in the traditional stories of the Pacific Northwest?

Chapter Eight gives some specific suggestions for meditating on the essence of an animal mask outside of the ritual itself. In addition, if you are working with the animal powers, try keeping a notebook in writing and drawing about them. What are your own associations with the creatures of the following? How and when do you interact with their living manifestations? Which ones appear most often in your thoughts or dreams? What are they saying or doing?

Done this way, the masked rites can not only connect you with their archaic powers but help you develop a more truly earth-based spiritual path. The mythos you help to manifest will be allied to its cultural roots, yet drawing upon the strength of its land-roots.

Notes

1. For an introduction to the subject of ancient inscriptions in North America, see Barry Fell, *America B.C.* (New York: Quadrangle, 1976). For a more detailed, nuanced study of the Celtic inscriptions, see William R. McGlone et al., *Ancient American Inscriptions* (Sutton, MA: Early Sites Research Society, 1993).

2. Carol Lee Sanchez, "New World Tribal Communities," *Weaving the Visions: Patterns in Feminist Spirituality*, Judith Plaskow and Carol Christ, eds. (San Francisco: Harper & Row, 1989), 346.

3. How to find your power animal is explained in Cook, Angelique S., and G. A. Hawk. *Shamanism and the Esoteric Tradition.* (St. Paul, MN: Llewellyn, 1992); in Chas S. Clifton, ed., *Witchcraft Today Book 3: Witchcraft and Shamanism* (St. Paul, MN: Llewellyn, 1994); and in Michael Harner, *The Way of the Shaman* (San Francisco: Harper & Row, 1980).

4. Spider Redgold, "Southland Learnings," *Woman of Power* 19 (Winter 1992): 76–77.

Chapter Eight

Making the Masks

Ready-made masks might be found at costumers' or import and folk-art shops, but the prices will usually be high for masks that are actually made to wear rather than merely hang on the wall for decoration. In addition, such masks may not stand up to the rough handling they will doubtlessly get by being carried to and from the working site. Papier-mâché masks will take a fair amount of rough handling, and if damaged are easily repaired. The main drawback to papier-mâché masks is their weight; they tend to be on the heavy side. Masks of Stag and Mare tend to be much larger than the others, which need be no more than full-facial ones.

Another thing to consider is that it might be wise to put off making elaborate masks of papier-mâché or other permanent materials, or buying expensive custom-made masks, until your group has gained some experience with the rites. Instead of jumping in straightaway, take a gradual approach. You never know if the people concerned in forming the initial shamanistic group will take to this type of working. As the idea of working this way becomes more formalized and established, a common pool of masks can be established. For a few friends getting together to try a shamanistic working for the first time, or indeed any group wanting to try a rite wearing masks, the easiest masks to make are the simple cardboard or stiff-paper ones.

Cut-Out Paper Masks

Cut-out cardboard or paper masks are not all that strong and will, at best, last for one or two meetings, but their attraction is that they are simple and quick to make. Perhaps more importantly, they begin to give the wearer something of the feel and atmosphere that goes with working masked.

Cut-out masks may be made inexpensively from a variety of stiff papers or light cardboard (1). You probably have something in your home that will work: lightweight boxes, food cartons, wrapping paper, large envelopes, paper shopping bags, or something of that sort. From this you can create a simple mask in one of two ways.

One method is to draw the face shape on the paper as shown (2), then cut it out with scissors. Fold it in half lengthwise and mark the position of the eyes (3). Using a knife with the mask laid flat, cut the eyes out. With the mask still flat, draw on the mask the animal or bird face the wearer has adopted for the rite (4).

Finally, cut two wide strips from the remains of the card (5). Staple one

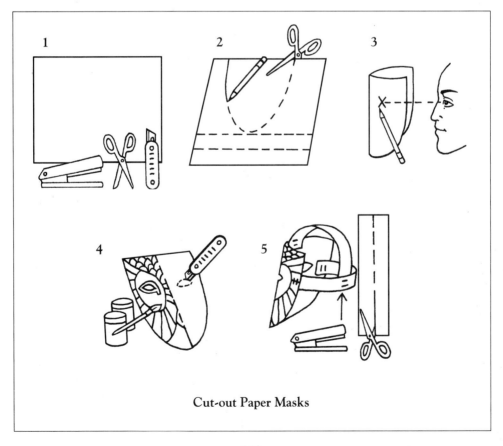

Cut-out Paper Masks

of the strips to the edge of the mask at or just below eye level. Pass the free end of the strip around the head to get the right length, cut, and staple. A second strip is stapled to the top center of the mask; then it is passed over the top of the head and down to the horizontal strip, where it is marked, cut, and stapled. The end product is something like an ice hockey goalie's mask. It is now ready to wear for the rite.

Alternatively, fold the paper or cardboard in half lengthwise first, then cut away one corner of the folded edge to make room for your nose. Draw the outline you want and cut away both thicknesses at once so that the mask will be symmetrical when you unfold it. This type of mask will rest chiefly on the nose and cheeks; add string or elastic to hold it in place. Eyeglass wearers could even tape it to a spare pair of glasses.

Paper masks can be decorated with poster paints, plus glued-on feathers, fur, fringe, and other appropriate decorations. Horns, whiskers, ears, and other features are easily added. Beaks and snouts can be made from additional folded pieces of paper affixed to the face mask by arrangements of tabs and slots, glue, or tape. Although they will not stand up to rough usage, paper masks can express the essence of any of the animals depicted in the masked rites. For more ideas on how to create individual animal masks, a good resource book is Michael Grater's *Paper Mask Making*.

Papier-Mâché Masks

For a more solid and longer-lasting version of the cardboard mask, a papier-mâché one takes a lot of beating. A good way to start is by using a balloon to support the papier-mâché layers as they are added. The great advantage to this method is that the balloon gives you the basic face shape plus a bonus: after cutting, you are left with two masks. In addition, the balloon method gives you a second option. Instead of creating simple face masks, with careful cutting you can create a helmet mask which can then be horned.

Since the balloon mask begins as a basic featureless face-shaped mask, the features that make up the persona of the mask are made out of cardboard or block polystyrene and glued to the mask. When glued into position, they too can be given two or three layers of papier-mâché to strengthen and blend them into the body of the mask.

For the mask, you will need a balloon, newspaper, flour or cellulose paste, petroleum jelly (such as Vaseline) or liquid detergent, and a paste brush (1). First, blow up the balloon to approximately the size of your head and tie off the neck with a piece of string below the knot as a further precaution against air leakage (2). Cover the balloon with either a coat of Vaseline or

soap to prevent the papier-mâché from sticking to it as it dries (3).

Cut the paper into squares, dip the squares into the paste, and start pasting them over the balloon (4), making sure they overlap each other, giving the mask more strength. When the first layer is finished, start the second layer of paste-soaked paper, gradually building up to about four or five layers.

Next, hang the balloon up to dry by the string (5), making sure that it is well away from any fires or radiators. I always leave mine for about three days before working on it to make sure that it is thoroughly dry. If the mask is going to be a facial one rather than the helmet type, the casting is next cut in half (which pops the balloon, of course!) and trimmed to fit snugly over the face.

Holding the mask up to your face will give you some idea of where to position the eye-holes (6). Mark and then cut the holes out with a sharp craft knife. Glue on any features you wish to add (7) and give the whole mask one final layer of paper to bind the whole lot together more firmly. You may wish to use a paper slightly heavier than newspaper for the final layer. Finally, fix the elastic or string through holes made in the mask at eye level and adjust them to hold the mask firmly in place (8).

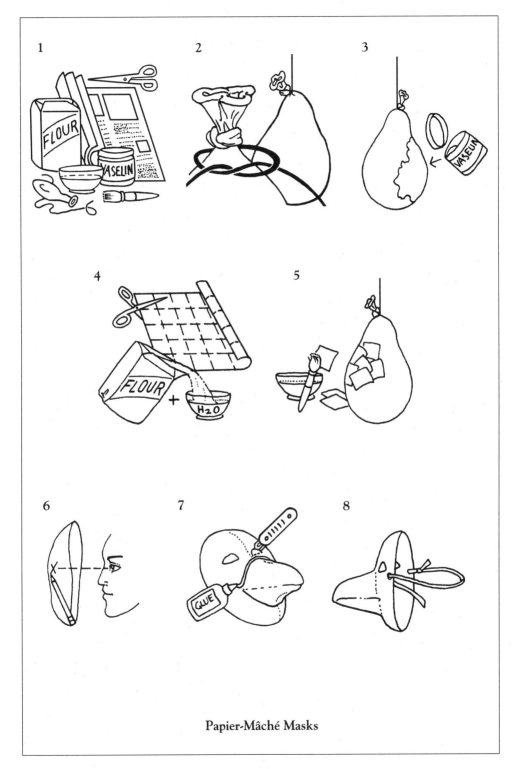

Papier-Mâché Masks

Alternative

Using the basic balloon shape once again, you can make what I consider to be a better type of mask, the helmet mask. Proceed through steps 1–5. Instead of cutting the balloon in half, starting at the hole left by the popped balloon, cut a section out extending to about half-way up the mask (6–7, page 145). Hold it against your face to help you decide how much more you will have to cut away. Trim small but equal amounts from the side and the top of the mask while trying it against the face constantly. Eventually the mask will be trimmed enough to allow it to slip over the head and face. Mark and cut the eye-holes. Finally, the rather pointed chin end can be shortened and given a more rounded shape.

Again, cardboard or block polystyrene can be used for the mask's features. They are then glued to the mask, which is given another layer or two of papier-mâché.

For some masks, such as Stag's, you will have to build up a deer-like muzzle separately. Make a mold of clay or plasticine, cover it with petroleum jelly, cut some tissue paper into small strips, making sure they overlap when sticking them to the greased mold. Next, build up the shape with three or four layers of papier-mâché, then leave it to thoroughly dry. Finally, ease it off the mold.

Draw a pencil line down the center of the mask, and do the same with the feature you are adding then trim off around the edge of the casting to fit the mask. Using the pencil lines as a guide, stick the feature to the mask with either gummed paper or masking tape. Putting the mask on, check that it looks right. If it does, then build up another two or three layers of papier-mâché strips over the joint to bond and blend the two together. As a personal preference, I then give the mask another layer for extra strength. The edges of the mask should be sealed with glue; a "white glue" such as Elmer's, diluted 50/50 with water, will suffice.

You can paint your mask with either poster paints or, as I prefer, powder paints mixed with a flour and water paste, leaving each coat to dry and harden before painting again.

With the balloon method, you may mold and add all the features needed for any of the thirteen masks separately, then add them to the basic shape. I have also seen balloon masks used where the bird or animal face was painted directly on the mask, which had first been colored with a matte-white emulsion. It was pretty effective, too!

The most striking use I have ever seen a balloon molding put to was as a helmet headdress for a priestess. Careful cutting created a close-fitting helmet that left her face clear. From a plasticine mold shaped to fit the helmet, she made a pair of ram's horns that when glued into position followed the curve of the helmet, with the tips of the horns just under her ear lobes.

The rest of her headdress was covered in small breast feathers glued into place individually. She sprayed the helmet with a couple of coats of silver paint—the end result: a ritual headdress!

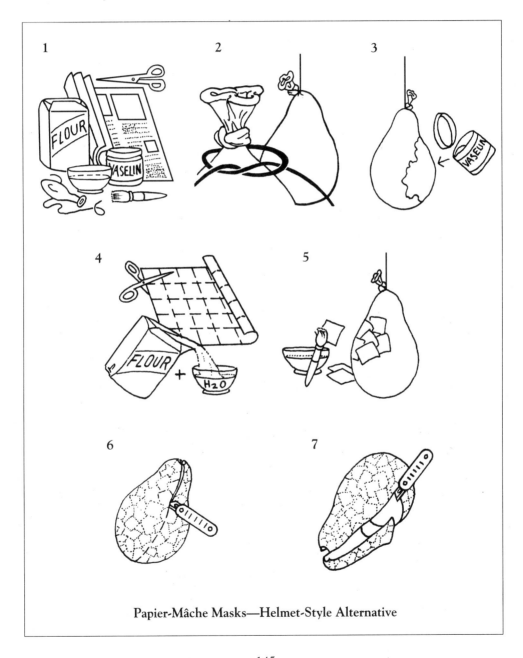

Papier-Mâche Masks—Helmet-Style Alternative

The Plaster Mask

This mask is modeled on the wearer's own face. Two or three people are needed for the mask-making process. The materials list includes petroleum jelly (such as Vaseline), two to three rolls of plaster bandages, a strip of cotton cloth about 2 x 24 inches, newspapers or paper towels, a roll of plastic food wrap, a bowl of lukewarm water, and a container to hold the strips (1).

The model must first coat her or his face with petroleum jelly from throat to hair line and lie down in a comfortable position, for they must be motionless for at least half an hour. The mask-makers should lay a sheet of plastic wrap across the model's eyes, sealing it with Vaseline so that water will not drip into the eye sockets. Men with mustaches and beards should also cover them with plastic wrap so that the bandages don't stick.

The cotton strip goes across the eyes and extends out to the sides, so that it will eventually become a tie to help hold the mask on the wearer's head.

The workers should now dip several plaster strips into water and lay them on sheets of newspaper to drain. Do not let them become wrinkled; as soon as the plaster gets damp, it sets within minutes. Once placed, it cannot be repositioned.

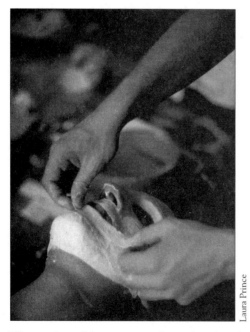

Laura Prince

The mask-maker positions plaster bandage strips across the model's face.

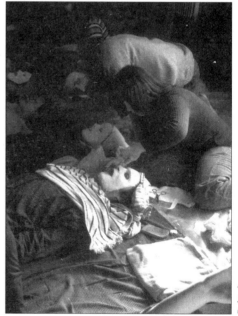

Robin Larsen

Plaster mask-making requires a good deal of floor space and several pairs of hands.

146

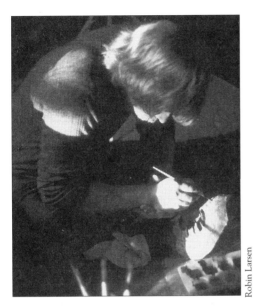

Plaster masks can be painted as desired.

When the mask-making is finished, the model must continue to lie still until the mask is dry enough that it feels solid. Try to loosen it first at the chin and temples, but make sure that it has hardened to rigidity before removing it. Once it is off, hold it to the light to check for weak spots that require reinforcement.

The mask should be allowed to dry for at least twelve more hours. Seal its edges with diluted white glue, trim away ragged bits, and sand the mask as desired. Eye-holes may be carefully cut with a knife—support the mask from below with a towel while cutting into it.

At this point, the mask may be painted and decorated as desired. Don't rush—let one coat of paint dry completely before starting another one.

Start building the mask from the edges inward. Go ahead and build layers over the eyes—openings will be cut later. Leave nostril holes for the model to breathe through. For projecting animal beaks or snouts, make a layer of plaster bandage, add a cardboard shape as needed, and then layer more bandages over it to blend it into the mask.

Do not go far below the chin, or the mask will be difficult to remove. Smooth the wet bandages with the fingers to cut down the amount of sanding needed later. For some masks, it may be enough to come down only as far as the wearer's upper lip.

A solid mask requires at least three layers of bandages. Alternate the layers' directions—horizontally, vertically, circularly—for greater strength.

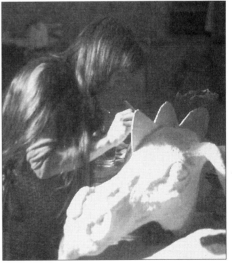

The plaster mask technique allows creative things to happen.

147

Molded Masks

If you need a mask that does not follow the contours of your face but stands out from it, you have other options. One is to make a mold. For this you will need such things as plasticine, Vaseline, newspaper cut into 1–2 inch squares, cellulose or flour paste, paste brush, and a board for modeling on (1). The materials available are quite varied—visit a good art-supply or hobby store and look at the sculpture section. You may find different types of clay and modeling compounds, instant papier-mâché, and other useful materials.

The first step is to draw the outline of a full-sized face on the board (2). If your plasticine is hard, soften it in warm water, drying it off afterwards.

Working to your outline, start to build up the mask with the plasticine (3–4). Remember to keep the features bold, but simple. The last thing you want is a lot of intricate details. When you are satisfied with your mask mold, the next step is to grease it with Vaseline and cover it with squares of tissue paper (5). Start applying the squares of newspaper, having first soaked them in water, making sure the squares overlap each other; then paste.

Using both the fingers and the paste brush, make sure that the papier-mâché follows the details of the mold. Pasting layer after layer, build the mask up to either five or six layers. Keeping it well away from fires or radiators, let the mask dry thoroughly before removing it from the mold

Before painting the mask, check for damage and repair any tears with glue and paper. When it comes to decorating, a coat of emulsion makes a good base for further painting with poster colors. The final step is to fix tape or elastic to the sides of the mask level with the eye-holes (6), adjusting them to hold the mask in place without being too tight or uncomfortable.

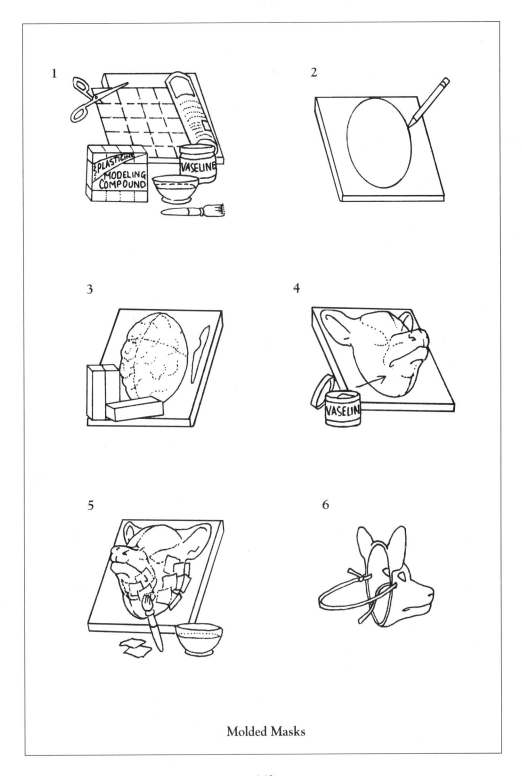

Molded Masks

Wire-Frame Masks

For the really ambitious, one of the best ways of making a total head mask is the wire-frame method. In this case, you will need soft, easily bent wire (1). Start by drawing the outline of the mask on paper (2), then bend some of the wire around the outline (3).

Next, start creating the framework by twist-joining a series of loops to the outline wire, making sure the one at the base is big enough to fit over the head (4). It is the loops that round out the mask, so they must be carefully bent to shape and spaced every two and a half inches along the wire outline frame.

Before starting to cover the frame, check that there are no sharp wire ends

sticking out and that the whole frame is firm. It is also a good idea to check that you can see out from where the eye-holes are going to be, and if necessary, twist in more wire to frame them.

To cover the frame, you can use either strips of gummed paper or plaster of Paris bandage (6). With the pre-glued paper strip, it is just a question of wetting the strip, looping it around the wire, and passing it over the frame until it is covered. More layers of gummed strips can be added until the maker feels satisfied that the skin of paper is thick enough to stand the rough and tumble of a ritual working. Then paint the mask as you wish (7).

These are just a few of the many ways of making ritual masks.

Philadelphia Mummers' Museum

Modern Mummers' wire-frame masks and headdresses are a carryover from earlier times when the technique was used by traveling troupes of masked entertainers.

Wire-Frame Masks

With a wire-frame mask covering your head, you are in effect turning the clock back to the age of the old mummers. Frowned upon and eventually suppressed by the church, the traveling troupes of masked entertainers performing Christianized plays were in fact carrying on a far older tradition. Presenting religious beliefs in the form of a play, a practice well known in the Pagan mystery traditions, originated in the far-older shamanistic tribal or clan gathering, when such rites were used to try to influence the spirits of the dead to help the living. We have only to look at the mummers and their masks illustrated in the Luttrel *Psalter*, a fourteenth-century book of psalms. Most of the masks shown there would look more at home in a Pagan rather than a Christian setting, leading me to think that the masks themselves were a carry-over from earlier times, while the plays and dances portrayed Christianity much in the same way as a Passion play does today.

"Charging" the Mask

A ritual mask is more than just a theatrical prop. On the island of Bali, which has an exceptionally rich heritage of masked religious drama, an actor will spend considerable time before a performance contemplating the mask that he will wear. He sits holding the mask and looking at it until he begins to feel that he is looking at his own face. Even his breathing changes, matching itself with the bodily tempo of the character—god, demon, hero, animal—of the mask. Only then will he be ready to wear the mask.[2]

Once your mask is prepared, therefore, more magical work remains to be done. The Balinese go through an elaborate consecration ritual that can last ten days, in which the appropriate energy is brought into the mask. Once the consecration is finished, the mask is stored in a cloth bag inside a basket in the temple.[3] The Balinese and other traditional mask-using cultures realize that ritual masks can and do radiate psychic power and therefore are not meant for public display. If you are going to enter the masked rites, you must ask under what, if any, circumstances you would display your mask, sell your mask, or destroy your mask

One Craft method of preparation is a little like the Balinese technique. It is a variant of scrying for visions in a magical mirror, but instead of a convex mirror, a regular flat mirror is used. Having the room fairly dark, except for one or two candles or other soft light glowing on the wearer's face, will make this technique more effective.

Begin by looking at your own face in a mirror hung at a convenient height or held steadily by your working partner as you sit facing one another. Having a partner enables you to conduct a dialogue with the mask without the risk of feeling self-conscious about "talking to yourself."

Put on your mask and watch its reflection in the mirror. While you do so, your partner may speak to the mask, using words something like these: "Hello, Raven (or whomever). Here is a mirror for you to look in. I call on you to join us and be welcome here."

Give the mask your voice: What would it say? (It may speak in words or in other sounds.) Watching in the mirror as the mask speaks and see through its eyes help to "charge" the mask, to

imbue it with the archetypal energy of its character. Again, watching the mask speak in the mirror helps to move you from "This is ordinary me wearing a mask" to "I speak as Raven" or to "Raven speaks this way."

As a supplement to the mirror technique, try propping the mask up in a dark place and setting a candle behind it to shine out its eyes, jack-o-lantern style. Think of "feeding" the mask with your energy. Honor it. The process of "charging" it is not an overnight one.

In the words of the British writer Nigel Aldcroft, "A fully empowered spirit mask generates an eerie presence

Robin Larsen

Charging a mask can be done before a mirror, in a variant of scrying for visions.

and power, often seeming like a non-human 'watcher' on the altar and becoming a focus for Otherworld forces, even more so when worn."[4]

Lastly, what happens when a mask is no longer needed? In many traditional cultures, they were simply destroyed, in a similar fashion to the way that a Navajo sand painting is erased after the curing ceremony for which it was created is finished. Other cultures buried masks or let them deteriorate in a protected natural spot. Any of these methods may seem perverse in our culture, in which "art objects" are restored, displayed, and protected indefinitely if possible, but the Craft does not live in a museum. We recognize our place in the cycles of birth and death, and should a mask no longer be of use, it too should be allowed to "die."

Perhaps in working masked once again we can recapture some of the old mystery and magic that in the past drew people to the Craft, even though discovery would have and often did mean death. When wearing even the simplest of masks we present a hidden face to the Goddess and the old Gods while magically changing our personality to suit the face the mask presents. Thus, with practice, the circle becomes not only the working circle, but the circle of transformation as well.

Notes

1. Michael Grater, *Paper Mask Making* (Mineola, NY: Dover Books, 1990). Originally published in Britain as *Paper Faces* (London: Milles & Boon, 1967).

2. "Lie and Glorious Adjective: An Interview with Peter Brook," *Parabola* VI.3 (August 1981), 63.

3. Judy Slattum, "The Living Masks of Bali," *Shaman's Drum* 34 (Spring 1994), 34.

4. Nigel Aldcroft, "Spirit Masks in European Paganism," *The Cauldron* 57 (Summer 1990), 2.

Chapter Nine

Robert Cochrane: Tregetour or Magician?

The "Masked Rites of Tubal Cain" derive from the coven headed by Robert Cochrane, a leading figure in the British Craft revival of the 1960s. In her book *The Rebirth of Witchcraft*,[1] Doreen Valiente gives us a fair and accurate picture of Robert Cochrane, the man, including his faults. Like the rest of us, he certainly had some. Valiente does not delve deeply into Cochrane, the magician, even though she makes the valid point that many of his rituals were more "shamanistic" than, for want of a better word, "formal" magic.

Many of Cochrane's ideas were innovative, yet seemingly based on historically proven fact. On the other hand, Cochrane did supply author Justine Glass with the totally spurious "1724" story, based on the numbers engraved on a copper plate that Doreen Valiente bought for him, which he then claimed had been handed down through his family for well over a hundred years. Glass' book, *Witchcraft the Sixth Sense—and Us*,[2] gave this story credence. When it became public knowledge, no one knew what to make of this man—and of what he claimed to be the traditional Craft. Yet they were still intrigued by Cochrane's "old tradition," which was so different from the better-known Gardnerian Craft.

Ever since Cochrane's death in 1966, many people have asked, "What would have happened had he lived longer?" meaning, of course, how much influence would he have had in shaping the future of Witchcraft? No one really knows, but, strangely enough, Cochrane partially answered that question in a letter to the late William G. Gray, the famous occult author and founder of the Sangreal rites. In it, Cochrane writes, "I keep on getting the feeling that we are preparing the ground for a crop that we will not reap, waiting for a dawn that may never come, but wait we must. We are the force for something else that is to occur, the creators of opinion for a new concept that is arising in this world."

As this excerpt shows, Cochrane never really expected to become the leader of a vast network of covens-within-the-clan, nor did he expect that what he believed in and taught as the Craft would reach others beyond his immediate coven. More than once he told me that if his teaching would reach further, it would have to be because of others rather than himself. My collaboration with Doreen Valiente, which produced *Witchcraft: A Tradition Renewed*, began this outreach by presenting the basic coven structures, tools, and rites. This book now brings the process a stage further, for

Cochrane himself never took the shamanistic rites this far, but worked them on a more or less *ad hoc* basis. I have taken his basic ideas and extended them to their present form because that is what logic dictated.

Apart from what he taught me, the only hard evidence concerning his works are letters. Perhaps the most revealing of all are those written to William G. Gray, whom he very much admired. Just before he died, Bill Gray passed them over to me to work on, which means that I am able to take ideas and concepts from them and enlarge on these while showing how they all interlock to give an overall picture of what Cochrane called his "traditional mysteries."

Before going on, let us consider the question posed by the title of this chapter. Was Cochrane a real magician of the old tradition, or was he just another magical trickster, a "tregetour" or mountebank who jumped on the occult bandwagon, as some people who never even met the man now claim that he did? Perhaps what is written here will serve to help people to make up their own minds about him and not prejudge or blindly accept everything claimed of both him and his works. During his lifetime his harshest critics often were those of us who had worked with him! Even then we had the feeling that what he did

Robert Cochrane

William G. Gray

was very different from the usual occult workings. So what was so special about the way he worked all those years ago?

First, unlike so many magical groups at that time, Cochrane's group preferred to work outdoors. Depending on what sort of ritual was being worked, it would be either on top of a hill or in a woodland clearing. For Cochrane, the hilltop was open to the four winds of the "Castle," which in turn represented the four elements, while working among trees produced a wilder form of nature magic more involving the God of vegetation and very different from the Goddess magic worked on the high and lonely hill.

He also advocated "cave magic," even though we only worked it in a limited way. An article that he wrote on working a cave ritual appeared in *New Dimensions* in the 1960s, and was later reprinted by Michael Howard in *The Cauldron*.[3] When I followed up on his thinking, to my surprise I found that the idea of a cave-and-cauldron ritual stemmed originally from an Anglo-Saxon Pagan concept; thus it could have been passed on to him from an older source. After all, on July 19, 1825, a report concerning the "swimming" of an alleged wizard appeared in the *London Times*, having first appeared in the *Suffolk Herald*. At Wickham-Skeith in Suffolk, Isaac Stebbins, who was rumored to have bewitched a thatcher's wife and a local farmer, volunteered to be "swum." Of course, as would happen in a small village, rumor begat rumor until in the end, every time something went wrong, poor old Stebbins got the blame for it. To clear himself, then, he asked to undergo the good old-fashioned test of being "swum" to establish his innocence—and this just before the start of the Victorian Age. Consequently, if the idea of swimming a person to establish their guilt or innocence on the charge of "witchcraft" was still accepted in some areas, we can legitimately ask what else lingered on in the somewhat-closed communities of the countryside.

When looking at Cochrane's life, another valid point to consider is that he and his wife at one time worked the narrow boats of the canals. If there ever was a "closed community," this was it, and Cochrane was one of the few outsiders to be accepted into it. During the latter half of the eighteenth century, when the explosion of canal-building hit Great Britain, families from the villages along the route of any canal would be pulled in to crew the barges, taking with them the folklore of their area. As more time passed, families were born, raised, and died on these narrow boats, and as time went by, the more the narrow-boat communities became isolated and inward-looking.

I believe that this milieu was where Cochrane obtained some of his material that did not conform to the 1960s pattern of Witch beliefs, garbled though it might have been through being handed down by word of mouth. It also explains why so many people think that he had rather an informal, simplistic set of traditions—to be honest about it, at first, this is what I thought, too. It was not until I started to clarify Cochrane's work as a magician for this chapter that I realized just what he had got and what he really meant when he said, "The threefold lamp is still waiting to be found," which only goes to prove that for years I could not see the wood for the trees—probably one of the most common occult failings that there is.

Even though there is no distinct boundary among them, Cochrane's workings must be looked at as falling into three separate traditions. First, there are the Mysteries of the Goddess, which are always worked on a hilltop. Second, the Mysteries of the Old Horned God and Lord of the Greenwoods, Robin Goodfellow, which are always held in the forest glade. Finally, there are the Mysteries of the Cave and Cauldron, which are always held underground and dedicated to the Triple Goddess aspected as Fate or Destiny. So, far from being a simplistic nature religion as some people think,

Cochrane's workings and concepts were more complex. Perhaps confusion arose because many of his concepts overlap or sometimes seem to contradict one another.

Cochrane always stressed that, beyond all the images we have of the old Gods and Goddesses, there is a primal energy or force we choose to call "Creation," who so ordained that the universe would come into being. Some call this force the Ultimate Goddess, while others call it God; and Cochrane in one of his letters called it the "unknown God." I prefer to think of this power as the unnamed Goddess, so remote and powerful that there is no way we can really understand Her, let alone get near Her. To do so would invite total oblivion, for she is the Alpha-Omega of all creation and destruction. Another name for her is Fate, or Destiny, and She will still be there after all Gods, Goddesses, humanity, and this world have perished. That matters very little to Her in Her remoteness, for at Her command the whole process of creation and life can be started again on another world somewhere else in this universe. If we liken this Godhead to a many-faceted jewel of which we are only able to see one face, it offers an explanation of why the Godhead can be all things spiritual, yet still remain the Godhead. Contradiction only creeps in when a religion or sect claims that the one face of the Godhead they can see is the only true one; by doing this, they diminish and belittle the Godhead itself.

In our case, we believe that the Godhead manifests itself in the aspect of the Goddess, the Horned God, and the Young Horned King—the mother, the father, and the child. The Goddess, first and foremost, is the Goddess of life, death, and rebirth; as the lunar Goddess, you will find all her faces portrayed in the phases of the Moon. The new Moon represents the young Maid; the full Moon, the mature Mother; the waning moon, the Old Hag; and the dark of the Moon, death and the hidden time before rebirth. Thus she is the Goddess of the seasons as well as Goddess of both life and death.

As the Pale-Faced Goddess of the North, she presides over the castle wherein is found the Cauldron of Rebirth, an aspect that Cochrane emphasized in his Ritual of the Castle. Based on an ancient myth and more suited to a single magician or a working couple rather than a large group, it demonstrates Cochrane's association of the Goddess with the top of a high and lonely hill where the four winds that represent the four elements can blow wild and free.

He balanced the feminine mysteries of the Goddess with those of the Old Horned God, Lord of the Greenwoods and God of fertility. Cochrane held that the real basis upon which the coven or "clan" was built was the divine aspect of the Dying God of vegetation, reborn again in the spring— the concept of the divine sacrificial king. When this ancient idea of the king who died in the May Eve rites to be replaced by a younger successor was modified for the coven, Cochrane maintained, the "magister" or "devil" of the clan remained the sacrificial king's equivalent. He would hold his coven office for seven years, after which he paid a price or penance before holding office for another seven.

His nominal subordinate was the "maid" of the coven. She balanced his masculinity and served as his partner in the rites. She could also take over from the magister if he started to go wrong. Such an event was not unknown in Cochrane's working group. At one time we were working on a problem of Bill Gray's, and, as Cochrane later wrote in a letter to Gray himself:

> As we ended (we started out much earlier than arranged because of various things), I offered the final actions and words that finish and hold the matter. In the middle of this, a form of words was used that normally constitutes a blessing, [but] to my horror I became conscious of extreme interfer-

ence that nearly changed the whole operation into a very dangerous curse. I began to use a form of words that would have reversed the whole thing....Jane spotted it and took over and finished the job.

Such is the power of the Maid. All coveners owed her absolute allegiance as the representative of the Goddess, while they owed to the Magister, the incarnate representative of the Deity, duty under the law which he represented.

When we turn to the concept of the Young Horned Child, we should remember that the whole mythos has changed considerably over the ages. The Child is no longer considered the offspring of an incestuous relationship between the Goddess and her brother, the Horned God, nor is he considered to be the spirit of the old God reborn into the body of the Young Horned King at the May Eve rites as part of the death and resurrection cycle. Instead, the Young Horned King has become the child born of the Goddess and named Truth and Beauty. He is represented at every coven meeting by the forked stang.

Cochrane's concepts about the stang were complex and multi-leveled. In his tradition, it could be read like a book from the bottom upwards. He described it like this:

160

Staff or stang: The horse. It is the supreme implement. It represents the middle pillar Yggdrasill; the Ash at one end, the Rowan at the other. Its roots are Malkuth, or the Gateway, that is physical experience, and at its top is the highest mystical experience. It should be forked and bound at the base with iron. [It is called] the Gateway because it is phallic and represents Hermes the Guide and divides into these aspects as it rises. [It is called] the Moon because it is the path to the mysteries. The foundation of wisdom and spiritual experience. It is love because it represents the union of male and female, therefore attraction and counter-attraction and is beauty the child of wisdom (horn child). It is death, the final transformation. The next attribute at the horns is the Goddess or the primal movement. In other words, it is a combination of masculine and feminine up to the position of death. Then it becomes the single path of enlightenment.

When we place the stang at the edge of the working circle and dress it with a garland, it serves as an altar to

Evan John Jones

A stang used by the author. Note the ram's head mounted on it. In certain rites a garland or other object might be suspended from the hook.

the Goddess and the old Horned God. In its function as the icon of the Young Horned King, it represents the son of the Goddess presiding over the rites of his Mother's worship. In sum, it expresses the concept of the Goddess, the Horned God, and the Horned Child.

When the cup is placed to the left of the stang, it symbolizes the Goddess and the feminine mysteries. Placed on the right, the knife represents the Old

161

Horned God and the masculine mysteries. Remove the cup and knife and replace them with a skull and crossbones at the foot of the staff, and it then becomes the symbol of total transformation in the cycle of death and resurrection. It may also stand for the transformation of non-initiate into Witch, which means, in effect, the death of a past way of life and the starting of a new one as a follower of the Old Religion.

Take away the skull and bones, replace them with a sickle, and you have the symbol of the Divine King dying on the tau cross of the Kerm

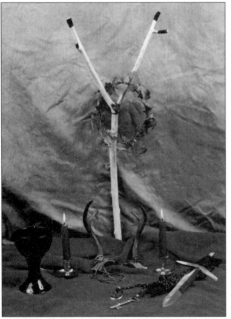

Wendy Crowe

This stang made from the forked branch of an ash tree, flanked by the cup on the left and knife on the right, and dressed with an ivy garland lends itself to ritual.

Oak, willingly sacrificing himself to the Old Gods to let the young king reign. These and other symbolic readings of the stang all lead back to the point from which they sprang: the mythos of the Young Horned Child born of the Goddess and sired by the Old Horned God.

Cochrane's views on death and reincarnation were also highly individualistic. Whereas many occultists talk about these subjects in a rather vague way, he specifically differentiated between the after-death experience of the soul of a Pagan and the soul of a Witch.[4] In one of his letters he claimed:

> Now around the Castle winds the river of Time. It is this that distinguishes us from the quick and the dead. I suppose this is classically the Lethe. It is also the beginning of power and [a] distinguishing mark between a witch and a pagan, since a witch crosses the river [while] a pagan remains with the quick.

The letter goes on to discuss the meaning of the Ash Ring. In another letter, Cochrane categorically states:

> When I am dead, I shall go to another place that myself and my ancestors created. Without their work, it would not exist,

since, in my opinion, for many eons of time the human spirit had no abode, then by desire to survive created the pathway into the other worlds.

Though he states this as an article of faith, if it should be true, it explains the difference between the abode of the Pagan soul and that of the Witch. If the Pagan, in life, be-lieves in the Summerlands, then in death this is where the soul will go, because belief has created them. If any religion teaches its followers that there is such a thing as an afterlife—be it paradise, heaven, or what have you—then it must exist because belief must have created it. Conversely, any person who believes in nothing but the reality of life and who, in effect, denies the existence of the soul, must at death fall into the void of nonexistence because this is what he or she has willed. As Cochrane said, "Nothing is got by doing nothing, and whatever we do now creates the world in which we exist tomorrow. The same applies to death: what we have created in thought, we create in that other reality."

So just what is it that we both hope and believe that we have created in this other reality? It is none other than the Castle, or Avalon, the far-famed hall of the Pale-Faced Goddess and her Cauldron of Rebirth. The one place that is neither of the heavens nor the earth and can only be seen with the eyes of a visionary in the western seas just off the coast, illuminated by the rays of the setting sun as it slips away below the horizon. Dream-woven in the first instance by the mystics, bardic poets, and visionaries of old, this is where our souls go after death, there to await rebirth. To reach this castle, we have to cross the river that separates the soul of a Pagan from that of a Witch. Pagans have their Summerlands; we have our Castle of the Goddess.

Like so many of Cochrane's workings, the Castle ritual was shamanically oriented, a point also made by Doreen Valiente, who stressed that Cochrane's rituals were more informal and shamanic than those found in the Gardnerian tradition. Had anyone said that to Cochrane's face, though, he would have blown his top. In the early 1960s, when we worked together, the word "shaman" suggested only something from a rather "primitive" past, while we, on the other hand, were looking for something more spiritual. Cochrane would not have enjoyed the image of the shaman/witch; he saw himself rather as the grand master and leader/teacher of his clan, holding the Key of Kings.

Now that I look back, I see that we overlooked something important: no matter how splendid the rose, its roots are still anchored in the mud.

163

When its roots are removed from the mud, it will wither and die. When Cochrane worked his rituals using the Mill, instinct, and gut reaction as well as the power of ritual, we had results. In retrospect, we had all the basic components needed to develop a shamanic system within the "clan" structure and by so doing, find the rose at the top of the plant. That, indeed, was the motivation for this book. Cochrane, the innovator, planted a seed in my mind, and the more I worked using his techniques, the more I realized that they needed to be put on a more formal footing.

I often wonder, however, had he lived longer, would he have come around to the idea that the way of the shaman is a valid tool to find the pathway to the worlds of the spirit and the Old Gods? He had all the basic keys, after all; all he had to do was to bring himself to realize it.

Perhaps the biggest snag of all in dealing with Robert Cochrane, both as man and as magician, was his attitude of trying to baffle, bewilder, and mystify everyone he met, in order to prevent them from forming a clear opinion of him. He called this technique his "grey magic," and by using it on people, he claimed that it gave him power over them. Since they were never as sure about him as he was about them, they were therefore weaker than he. For

some reason or other, he seemed to want to be at loggerheads with most other occultists, and the idea of having some sort of power over people, no matter how slight, fascinated him. This explains the totally spurious "1724" myth that was revealed in Justine Glass' book *Witchcraft, the Sixth Sense—and Us*.

With the benefit of hindsight, I think that he was a very frustrated man, which manifested itself in an attitude of "I know something that you don't." Yet once you got to know him, you found yourself face to face with a friendly, interesting person who, once he had taken to you, was intensely loyal to you, come what may. When he made the effort, he was a good communicator who could capture your interest while communicating some pretty complex ideas. He was also the first occultist who told me to my face that a lot of what he had done started off as sheer trickery, and that there was a good magical reason for this. Magic is the art of creating an "illusion" which eventually becomes reality. The masks mentioned in these pages are nothing more than the masks of illusion which, when used in a ritual way, become the reality of the soul.

More prosaically, the actual "clan" workings Cochrane conducted were experientially successful. After you experienced one, the one thing that you could say about them was that you had been to a real Witch meeting. Things used to happen, and more than once everyone had the distinct feeling that we were not alone, that others from the past had joined us. This was not because of anything visible; rather it was a feeling that people had in their bones. The feast after the ritual really was the "joyful feast" held under the stars in a place that had been declared sacred to the Old Ones. The very air itself felt charged with a potent energy, which bubbled with a sense of fun as well as with a sense of achieving what we set out to do: to raise the old power. We all knew what it felt like to be one of "Diana's darling crew," because we had really lived it. "Traditional witch" or not, Cochrane and his ways lifted us to this pitch. Other rituals that I have worked with other groups have been enjoyable and satisfying, but none of them managed to create the same atmosphere that his did. Some essential spark was missing, and I suppose that this elusive spark is what Cochrane's magic was really all about.

Some people who never experienced his rituals themselves have suggested that our feelings simply resulted from autosuggestion, that we were all susceptible to anything that he suggested might happen. This simply is not

true. For a start, some very well-known occultists from other disciplines attended most of his early meetings, and they picked up the same things as we novices did. With their experience, they should have spotted straight away when a snow job was being worked on them. Second, Cochrane himself was never quite sure what, if anything, would happen during the ritual. The only information people were given dealt with the mechanics of the rite and nothing else. Any discussion about what should or should not have manifested itself during the working took place afterward, informally.

All good things come to an end, unfortunately, and later in his magical career Cochrane, like so many others in a similar position, fell into a trap of his own making. He began to believe in his own myth, and when that belief began to intrude into his life outside the circle, it led eventually to his downfall. Being the grand master inside the circle is one thing, but trying to be the magister in the outside world is a sure recipe for disaster. He himself often said, "You cannot monkey with the buzz-saw." He did, and he paid for it.

When Cochrane died, I think that the Craft itself was the loser in many ways, yet I always return to what he wrote in another letter to Bill Gray: "I keep on getting the feeling that we are preparing the ground for a crop that we shall not reap."

Today, more people are interested in Cochrane's "family tradition" than ever were when he was living.

He also left behind another puzzle: was he one of the few remaining hereditary Witches, or was he just an out-and-out fake? In my opinion, if he was not an hereditary Witch with a handed-down lore, then he must have known someone who was, because so many of his ideas and concepts hark back to a very different form of the Craft than modern-day Wicca. Cochrane's usual public line was, "I am the last in a long line of hereditary Witches," but in one letter to Gray he dropped an interesting hint about something else: "I myself am a master of a small clan, the devil in fact. I in turn recognize the authority of others who are higher than myself, and that authority, once stated, is absolute." In the same letter he goes on to say, "We may be the last of the old school, but we still uphold the old attitudes and expect the same things. Above we two rises another authority whose writ is far older than ours, to that authority we give absolute allegiance."

Had this been written for public consumption, it could be claimed that he was inventing a "hidden leadership" as a way of boosting his own status, the old "I know something you don't" syndrome, but it was not. It was written in a private letter to Gray, and had Gray not later passed the letter on, no one else would have known anything of Cochrane's claim to be under a "higher authority." If he was only boosting his status, why tell just one person when he could just as easily have shouted it from the rooftops with far more effect?

In the final analysis, perhaps he was telling Gray obliquely what many people had suspected for a long time, that his Craft tradition did not come down to him through his family as he often claimed. Instead, during his travels around the country he was introduced to the Craft by a few remaining old-timers who held what was left of the old lore. On the other hand, he could quite easily have been what he claimed to be, and the "higher authority" claim could be just another example of his "grey magic," which made it impossible to be really sure just what he was. The truth he took to the grave with him, leaving many people wondering about the real Robert Cochrane: magister...or tregetour?

Notes

1. Doreen Valiente, *The Rebirth of Witchcraft* (London: Robert Hale, 1989).

2. Justine Glass, *Witchcraft, the Sixth Sense—and Us* (London: Neville Spearman, 1965).

3. Robert Cochrane, "The Witches' Esbat," *The Cauldron* 63 (Winter 1992), 6–8. [First published in 1964.]

4. Unlike many contemporary Witches, Cochrane used these two words differently. He once wrote, "Genuine witchcraft is not paganism, though it retains the memory of ancient faiths," adding that it was "the last real mystery cult alive." (Quoted in Valiente, 121.)

5. Valiente, 125.

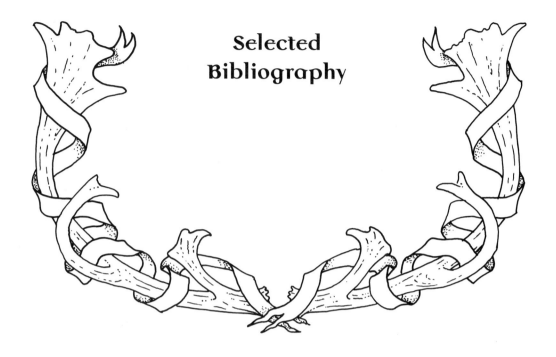

Selected Bibliography

Cawte, E. C. *Ritual Animal Disguise*. Cambridge: D. S. Brewer Ltd., 1978.

Clifton, Chas S., ed. *Witchcraft Today, Book Three: Witchcraft & Shamanism*. St. Paul, MN: Llewellyn Publications, 1994.

Cook, Angelique S., and G. A. Hawk. *Shamanism and the Esoteric Tradition*. St. Paul, MN: Llewellyn Publications, 1992.

Frank, Vivien, and Deborah Jaffé. *Making Masks*. Secaucus, NJ: Chartwell Books, 1992.

Frazer, Sir James. *The Golden Bough*. Abridged edition. New York: MacMillan, 1922 [1890].

Glass, Justine. *Witchcraft, the Sixth Sense—and Us*. London: Robert Hale, 1989.

Gover, Robert. *Voodoo Contra*. York Beach, ME: Samuel Weiser.

Grater, Michael. *Paper Mask Making*. Mineola, NY: Dover Publications, 1984 [1967].

Graves, Robert. *The White Goddess*. New York: Farrar, Straus and Giroux, 1948.

Grimes, Ronald L. "The Life History of a Mask." *The Drama Review* 36.3 (Fall 1992), 61–77.

Hansen, Jens Peder Hart, Jørgen Melgaard, and Jørgen Nordqvist, eds. *The Greenland Mummies*. Washington: Smithsonian Institution Press, 1991.

Hutton, Ronald. *The Pagan Religions of the Ancient British Isles: Their Nature and Legacy*. London: Blackwell, 1991.

Jones, Evan John, with Doreen Valiente. *Witchcraft: A Tradition Renewed*. London: Robert Hale, 1990.

Keickhefer, Richard. *Magic in the Middle Ages*. Cambridge: Cambridge University Press, 1989.

Larsen, Stephen. *The Mythic Imagination: Your Quest for Meaning through Personal Mythology*. New York: Bantam, 1990.

Lévi-Strauss, Claude., trans. Sylva Modelski. *The Way of the Mask*. Vancouver: Douglas & McIntyre, 1979.

Merrifield, Ralph. *The Archaeology of Ritual and Magic*. New York: New Amsterdam Books, 1988.

Napier, A. David. *Masks, Transformation, and Paradox*. Berkeley: University of California Press, 1986.

Paris, Ginette. trans. Joanna Mott. *Pagan Grace: Dionysos, Hermes, and Goddess Memory in Daily Life*. Dallas: Spring Publications, 1990.

———. trans. Gwendolyn Moore. *Pagan Meditations: Aphrodite, Hestia, Artemis*. Dallas: Spring Publications, 1986.

Pennick, Nigel. *Practical Magic in the Northern Tradition*. Wellingborough, Northamptonshire: The Aquarian Press, 1987.

Permet, Henry. *Ritual Masks: Deceptions and Revelations*. trans. Laura Grillo. Studies in Comparative Religion, ed. Frederick M. Denny. Columbia, SC: University of South Carolina Press, 1992.

Richardson, Alan. Earth God Rising. St. Paul, MN: Llewellyn Publications, 1990.

Sivan, Carole. *Maskmaking*. Worcester, MA: Davis Pubs., 1986.

Valiente, Doreen. *The Rebirth of Witchcraft*. London: Robert Hale, 1989.

———. *Witchcraft For Tomorrow*. London: Robert Hale, 1979.

Vulcanescu, Romulus. "Ritual Masks in European Cultures." *Encyclopedia of Religion*. New York: Macmillan, 1987.

Lewis-Williams, J. David. *Believing and Seeing: Symbolic Meanings in Southern San Rock Paintings*. London: Academic Press, 1981.

Young-Laughlin, Judy and Charles D. Laughlin. "How Masks Work, or Masks Work How?" *Journal of Ritual Studies* 2.1, 56–89.

Index

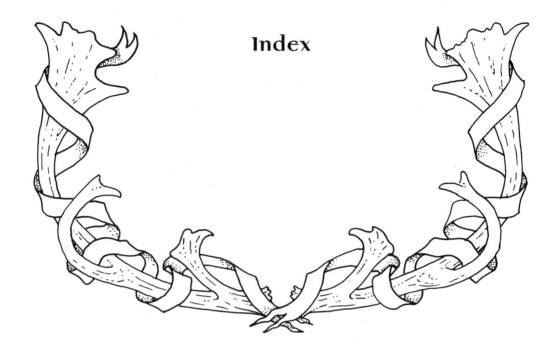

Illustration Credits

An effort has been made to trace ownership and/or copyright holder of all illustrations included in this book. We apologize for any errors or omissions. Upon notification, we will make appropriate acknowledgements in subsequent editions.

Illustrations are listed by page number, from top to bottom and left to right.

Page xxi—from cave drawing at Les Trois Frères. xxiii—Philadelphia Mummers Museum. 2—Margaret A. Murray, *God of the Witches*. 3—Margaret A. Murray, *God of the Witches*. 5—Eighteenth-century tarot card. 7—Photo © Malcolm Brenner, Eyes Open. 8—Photo by Robin Larsen. 9—Photo by Robin Larsen, mask made by Lauren Raine. 11—Photo © Malcolm Brenner, Eyes Open. 13—Margaret A. Murray, *God of the Witches*. 14—Photo © Malcolm Brenner, Eyes Open. 19—Photo by Jeff Farnum. 21—Photo by Karen St. Pierre. 24—Carrie Westfall. 25—Photo by Chas S. Clifton, mask by Martin Anthony. 29—Carrie Westfall. 31—Photo and mask by Robin Larsen. 33—Carrie Westfall. 36—Carrie Westfall. 38—Photo and mask by Terry Dimant. 40—Carrie Westfall. 25—Photo and mask by Karen St. Pierre. 43—Carrie Westfall. 46—Carrie Westfall. 47—Photo by Chas S. Clifton, mask by Martin Anthony. 49—Carrie Westfall. 52—Carrie Westfall. 55—Carrie Westfall. 58—Carrie Westfall. 59—Photo by Robin Larsen, mask made by Robin Larsen. 61—Carrie Westfall. 64—Carrie Westfall. 68—Tom Grewe. 69—Tom Grewe. 72—Tom Grewe. 75—Carrie Westfall. 78—Philadelphia Mummers Museum. 80—Margaret A. Murray, *God of the Witches*. 83—Photo © Malcolm Brenner, Eyes Open. 86—Tom Grewe. 91—Tom Grewe. 92—Photo © Malcolm Brenner, Eyes Open. 93—Photo by Evan John Jones. 101—Photo by Jeff Farnum. 109—Carrie Westfall. 110—Photo by Evan John Jones. 125—Photo by Robin Larsen. 131—Margaret A. Murray, *God of the Witches*. 133—Margaret A. Murray, *God of the Witches*. 140—Carrie Westfall. 143—Carrie Westfall. 145—Carrie Westfall. 146—Photo by Laura Prince. Photo by Robin Larsen. 147—Photo by Robin Larsen. Photo by Stephen Larsen. 149—Carrie Westfall. 150—Philadelphia Mummers Museum. 151—Carrie Westfall. 153—Photo by

Robin Larsen. 157—Personal photos, uncredited. 161—Photo by Evan John Jones. 162—Photo by Wendy Crowe.

Stay in Touch...
Llewellyn publishes hundreds of books on your favorite subjects

On the following pages you will find listed some books now available on related subjects. Your local bookstore stocks most of these and will stock new Llewellyn titles as they become available. We urge your patronage.

ORDER BY PHONE

Call toll-free within the U.S. and Canada, **1–800–THE MOON.**

In Minnesota call **(612) 291–1970.**

We accept Visa, MasterCard, and American Express.

ORDER BY MAIL

Send the full price of your order (MN residents add 7% sales tax) in U.S. funds to :

**Llewellyn Worldwide,
P.O Box 64383, Dept. K373-5
St. Paul, MN 55164–0383, U.S.A.**

POSTAGE AND HANDLING

- $4.00 for orders $15.00 and under
- $5.00 for orders over $15.00
- No charge for orders over $100.00

We ship UPS in the continental United States. We cannot ship to P.O. boxes. Orders shipped to Alaska, Hawaii, Canada, Mexico, and Puerto Rico will be sent first-class mail.

International orders: Airmail—add freight equal to price of each book to the total price of order, plus $5.00 for each non-book item (audiotapes, etc.).

Surface mail: Add $1.00 per item

Allow 4–6 weeks delivery on all orders. Postage and handling rates subject to change.

GROUP DISCOUNTS

We offer a 20% quantity discount to group leaders or agents. You must order a minimum of 5 copies of the same book to get our special quantity price.

Free Catalog

Get a Free copy of our color catalog, *New Worlds of Mind and Spirit*. Subscribe for just $10.00 in the United States and Canada ($20.00 overseas, first class mail). Many bookstores carry *New Worlds*—ask for it!

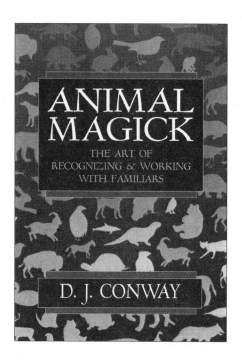

ANIMAL MAGICK
The Art of Recognizing & Working
with Familiars

D. J. Conway

The use of animal familiars began long before the Middle Ages in Europe. It can be traced to ancient Egypt and beyond. To most people, a familiar is a witch's companion, a small animal that helps the witch perform magick, but you don't have to be a witch to have a familiar. In fact you don't even have to believe in familiars to have one. You may already have a physical familiar living in your home in the guise of a pet. Or you may have an astral-bodied familiar if you are intensely drawn to a particular creature that is impossible to have in the physical. There are definite advantages to befriending a familiar. They make excellent companions, even if they are astral creatures. If you work magick, the familiar can aid by augmenting your power. Familiars can warn you of danger, and they are good healers.

Most books on animal magick are written from the viewpoint of the Native American. This book takes you into the exciting field of animal familiars from the European Pagan viewpoint. It gives practical meditations, rituals, and power chants for enticing, befriending, understanding, and using the magick of familiars.

1-56718-168-6, 256 pp, 6 x 9, softcover $13.95

ANIMAL-SPEAK
The Spiritual & Magical Powers
of Creatures Great & Small

Ted Andrews

The animal world has much to teach us. Some animals are experts at survival and adaptation, some never get cancer, some embody strength and courage while others exude playfulness. Animals remind us of the potential we can unfold, but before we can learn from them, we must first be able to speak with them.

In this book, myth and fact are combined in a manner that will teach you how to speak and understand the language of the animals in your life. *Animal-Speak* helps you meet and work with animals as totems and spirits—by learning the language of their behaviors within the physical world. It provides techniques for reading signs and omens in nature so you can open to higher perceptions and even prophecy. It reveals the hidden, mythical, and realistic roles of 45 animals, 60 birds, 8 insects, and 6 reptiles.

Animals will become a part of you, revealing to you the majesty and divine in all life. They will restore your childlike wonder of the world and strengthen your belief in magic, dreams and possibilities.

0–87542–028–1, 400 pp, 7 x 10, illus., photos, softcover   **$17.95**

DANCE OF POWER
A Shamanic Journey

Dr. Susan Gregg

Join Dr. Susan Gregg on her fascinating, real-life journey to find her soul. This is the story of her shamanic apprenticeship with a man named Miguel, a Mexican-Indian Shaman, or "Nagual." As you live the author's personal experiences, you have the opportunity to take a quantum leap along the path toward personal freedom, toward finding your true self, and grasping the ultimate personal freedom—the freedom to choose moment by moment what you want to experience.

Here, in a warm and genuine style, Dr. Gregg details her studies with Miguel, her travel to other realms, and her initiations by fire and water into the life of a "warrior." If you want to understand how you create your own reality—and how you may be wasting energy by resisting change or trying to understand the unknowable—take the enlightening path of the Nagual. Practical exercises at the end of each chapter give you the tools to embark upon your own spiritual quest.

Learn about another way of being ... *Dance of Power* can change your life, if you let it.

0-87542-247-0, 240 pp, 5 ¼ x 8, illus., photos, softbound $12.95

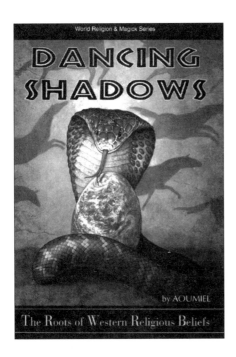

DANCING SHADOWS
The Roots of Western
Religious Beliefs

Aoumiel

At last, a contemporary Pagan perspective on Western religious history! Discover the historical roots of Neo-Paganism and its relationship to modern religions.

Learn the fascinating story of how the Pagan deities have been transformed and absorbed into the hierarchy of mainstream religions, and why Pagan beliefs have been borrowed, altered, and refuted by Aryan religions over the centuries. *Dancing Shadows* traces Western religions back 3,000 years to the Dravidian god/goddess beliefs of the ancient Indus Valley (which evolved into the Western Pagan tradition) and the patriarchal sky-god religion of the invading Aryans from Central Asia (on which modern Christianity, Judaism, and Islam are based). This book will show you how the cross-fertilization of these two belief systems—both traceable to a common religious ancestor—is the source of conflicts that continue today.

Aoumiel draws together current research in the fields of history, religion, archeology, and anthropology to formulate a cohesive theory for the origins of modern Neo-Paganism ... and presents a refreshing affirmation of the interconnection between all Western peoples and beliefs.

1-56718-691-2, 224 pp, 6 x 9, softcover $12.95

FINDING THE SACRED SELF
A Shamanic Workbook

Dr. Susan Gregg

Imagine what your life would be like if you felt totally safe at all times … loved unconditionally by all … and passion filled your every moment. Sound impossible? Finding and living from your sacred self is a profound act that can change the world. But how do you grab onto that sacred self which is your essence?

This book is about Dr. Susan Gregg's own process of stopping her inner pain and reclaiming her essential self. In her first book, *Dance of Power*, she described her apprenticeship with shamans Miguel and Sarita. Now, in *Finding Your Sacred Self*, she shares many of the exercises—which you can do alone or in a group—that helped her connect with her sacred self.

Through exercises such as "meeting your protector," "mirror meditations" and "channeling healing energies," you will actually experience your inner knowing. You will perceive the world in a whole new way. And you will finally come to remember the truth of who you are: joyous, intuitive, loving, and free.

1-56718-334-4, 240 pp, 6 x 9, softcover $12.00

HIS STORY
Masculinity in the
Post-Patriarchal World

Nicholas R. Mann

His Story was written for men of European descent who are seeking a new definition of being. The patriarchal worldview dominating Western thought has cut men off from the traditions which once directly connected them to the nature of their masculinity. This book offers them a means to locate and connect with their birthright—the "native tradition" that lives in the deepest core of their being—by drawing on the pre-Christian era's conception of a man's true masculine nature.

His Story contrasts patriarchal and pre-patriarchal ideas about masculine identity, self-definition, sexuality, symbology and spirituality—then provides a wealth of information on traditions and mythology that encompass many masculine archetypes, from those of the Grail legends to the Green Man, the Wild Man and the Horned God. Finally, the book reveals how men can connect again with these traditions and their own inherent source of personal power, thus transforming their relationships to those around them and to the world.

1-56718-458-8, 336 pp, 6 x 9, softcover $16.95

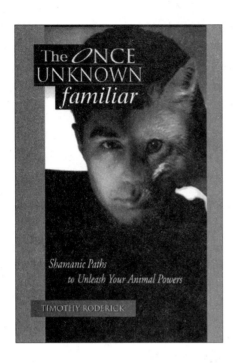

THE ONCE UNKNOWN
FAMILIAR
Shamanic Paths to Unleash
Your Animal Powers

Timothy Roderick

Discover the magical animal of power residing within you! Animal "Familiars" are more than just the friendly animals kept by witches—the animal spirit is an extension of the unconscious mind, which reveals its power to those who seek its help. By using the detailed rituals, meditations, exercises and journaling space provided within this workbook, you will tap into the long-forgotten Northern European heritage of the "Familiar Self," and invoke the untamed, transformative power of these magical beasts.

This book focuses on traditional Northern European shamanic means of raising power—including drumming, dancing and construction of animal "fetiches"—and provides a grimoire of charms, incantations and spells anyone can work with a physical animal presence to enhance love, money, success, peace and more.

This is the first how-to book devoted exclusively to working with physical and spiritual Familiars as an aid to magic. Get in touch with your personal animal power, and connect with the magical forces of nature to effect positive change in your life and the lives of those around you.

0–87542–439–2, 240 pp, 6 x 9, softcover $10.00

SHAMANISM AND THE ESOTERIC TRADITION

Angelique S. Cook & G.A. Hawk

Recharge and enhance your magical practice by returning to the source of the entire esoteric tradition—the shamanism of the ancient hunters and gatherers.

Whether you're involved in yoga, divination, or ritual magic, *Shamanism and the Esoteric Tradition* introduces you to the fundamental neo-shamanic techniques that produce immediate results. Shamanic practice is a tremendous aid in self-healing and personal growth. It also produces euphoria by releasing beta-endorphins, an effective antidote against depression.

The enormously powerful techniques presented here include inner journeys to find a power animal and teacher, past-life regression, healing methods, and journeys to help the dead. Gradually and properly used, shamanic power helps you generate positive synchronicities that can alter so-called "chance" life events, and enhance personal satisfaction, freedom and wholeness.

0-87542-325-6, 224 pp, 6 x 9, illus., index, softcover $12.95

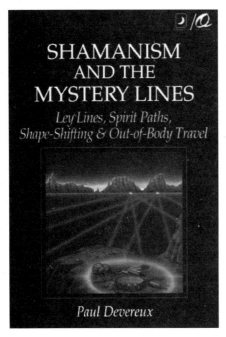

**SHAMANISM AND THE
MYSTERY LINES**
Ley Lines, Spirit Paths, Shape-Shifting
& Out-of-Body Travel

Paul Devereux

This book will take you across archaic landscapes, into contact with spiritual traditions as old as the human central nervous system and into the deepest recesses of the
human psyche. Explore the mystery surrounding "ley lines": stone rows, prehistoric
linear earthwork, and straight tracks in archaic landscapes around the world. Why
would the ancients, without the wheel or horse, want such broad and exact roads?
Why the apparent obsession with straightness? Why the parallel sections?

Are they energy lines? Traders' tracks? For those who have definite ideas as to what
a ley line is, be prepared for a surprise . . . and a possible shift in your beliefs about
this intriguing phenomenon.

The theory put forth and proved in *Shamanism and the Mystery Lines* is startling: that
all ancient landscape lines—whether physical manifestations as created by the
Amerindians or conceptual as in the case of Feng shui—are in essence spirit lines.
And underlying the concept of spirit and straightness is a deep, universal experience
yielded by the human central nervous system: that of shamanic magical flight—or
the out-of-body experience. This explanation is as simple and direct as the lines
themselves . . . flight is the straight way over land.

0-87542-189-X, 240 pp, 6 x 9, illus., softcover $12.95

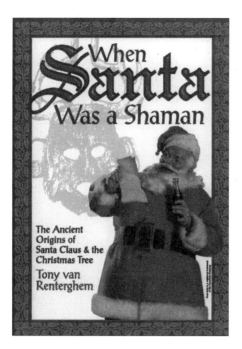

WHEN SANTA WAS A SHAMAN
Ancient Origins of Santa Claus and the Christmas Tree

Tony van Renterghem

This is an ancestral detective story, leading back to prehistoric times and man's first concepts of religion. The American Santa Claus (a revamping of the Dutch Saint Nicholas by an artist for the Coca-Cola company!) represents only the tip of a very ancient iceberg. Beneath it lies Western man's oldest stories : (1) the myth of the Tree of Fire, the last vestige of which is our Christmas Tree, and (2) the persistent, vague memory of the shaman, in harmony with Gaia, now transformed into a jolly old man with flying reindeer.

Learn how these stories were remembered around the world, camouflaged for safety and interwoven with other myths. Always resurfacing—in Holland and Belgium as Saint Nicholas (or more accurately Black Pete, the Dark Helper) and in Britain, Germany, France, Russia, Scandinavia, Spain, Italy, North Africa—these myths eventually crossed the Atlantic to America, where they were sanitized, commercialized and exported back into the world from which they came.

1-56718-765-X, 224 pp, 7 x 10, color illus., softcover $16.95

THE LLEWELLYN ANNUALS

Llewellyn's MOON SIGN BOOK: Approximately 500 pages of valuable information on gardening, fishing, weather, stock market forecasts, personal horoscopes, good planting dates, and general instructions for finding the best date to do just about anything! Articles by prominent forecasters and writers in the fields of gardening, astrology, politics, economics and cycles. This special almanac, different from any other, has been published annually since 1906. It's fun, informative and has been a great help to millions in their daily planning. New larger 5¼ x 8 format. **State year $6.95**

Llewellyn's SUN SIGN BOOK: Your personal horoscope for the entire year! All 12 signs are included in one handy book. Also included are forecasts, special feature articles, and an action guide for each sign. Monthly horoscopes are written by Gloria Star, author of *Optimum Child*, for your personal sun sign and there are articles on a variety of subjects written by well-known astrologers from around the country. Much more than just a horoscope guide! Entertaining and fun the year around. New larger 5 ¼ x 8 format. **State year $6.95**

Llewellyn's DAILY PLANETARY GUIDE: Includes all of the major daily aspects plus their exact times in Eastern and Pacific time zones, lunar phases, signs and voids plus their times, planetary motion, a monthly ephemeris, sunrise and sunset tables, special articles on the planets, signs, aspects, a business guide, planetary hours, rulerships, and much more. Large 5¼ x 8 format for more writing space, spiral bound to lie flat, address and phone listings, time-zone conversion chart and blank horoscope chart. **State year $9.95**

Llewellyn's ASTROLOGICAL POCKET PLANNER: Daily Ephemeris & Aspectarian: Designed to slide easily into a purse or briefcase, this all-new annual is jam-packed with those dates and planetary information astrologers need when forecasting future events. Comes with a regular calendar section, a smaller section for projecting dates into the year ahead, a 3-year ephemeris, a listing of planetary aspects, a planetary associations chart, a time-zone chart and retrograde table. **State year $7.95**

Llewellyn's ASTROLOGICAL CALENDAR: Large wall calendar of 48 pages. Beautiful full-color cover and full-color paintings inside. Includes special feature articles by famous astrologers, and complete introductory information on astrology. It also contains a lunar gardening guide, celestial phenomena, a blank horoscope chart, and monthly date pages which include aspects, Moon phases, signs and voids, planetary motion, an ephemeris, personal forecasts, lucky dates, planting and fishing dates, and more. 10 x 13 size. Set in Eastern time, with fold-down conversion table for other time zones worldwide. **State year $12.00**